KU-532-893

PART 1

Timeless Transformations

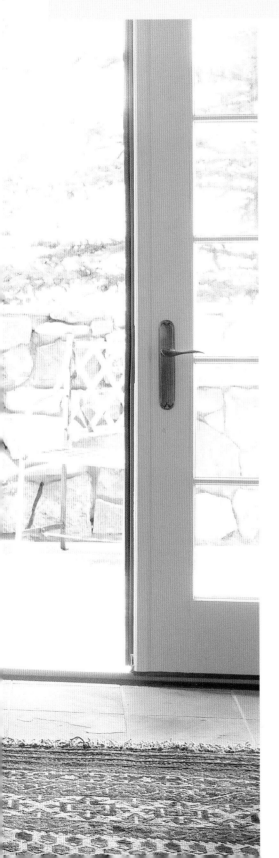

"Easy" is often difficult; even the simplest changes in the way a home looks and functions involve planning, a lot of head-scratching, and much detailed decision making. No remodel is ever as simple as just taking down a wall and merging two spaces, although the idea does seem simple enough. Questions arise immediately—if not by an architect, then certainly by a contractor. Are there structural issues? Windows to be removed or added? What about traffic flow—will you be moving a doorway? Will you be satisfied just patching the floor where that wall once stood? Or will you want to redo the entire floor in what was once two rooms? Note that wiring, plumbing, heating, and cooling may also be affected when a wall is removed. Yet the task itself is relatively simple.

Many such tasks can be done by homeowners who are handy, experienced, and prepared to commit time, energy, and patience to the job. But at some point even they usually defer to professionals—licensed plumbers and electricians, for example. Don't approach any home-remodeling project as a need to prove yourself. If you know what you want and, basically, how to get the job done, your value may lie in keen discernment: determining which pro to hire and being able to oversee the work that person needs to do.

How often have you heard, from friends or crestfallen colleagues, the complaint, "I couldn't be there all the time, so nothing was done right"? The truth is even if you are on the scene every day, mistakes can be made, right in front of your eyes, unless you know the drill: what's to be done and how to do it. Don't compete with the pros you hire, but make your needs are known. Never assume they understand what you're after until it is absolutely clear that they do. You need a contract that embraces every aspect of the job. What's more important, however, is to spell out, in writing—step by step—every need and preference. You and your remodelers must work together to achieve a common goal: getting the work done right. When everything falls into place as it should, even the hardest jobs will seem easier.

In the section that follows, you will find whole-house renovations and elegant additions that represent different levels of difficulty. But you will also find that each presents a rich variety of ideas and decorating tips that will be useful in any remodeling you undertake.

LEFT: The expansive new living room has high ceilings and a warm ambience.

Unboxed

Used as a ski chalet, this Beaver Creek, Colorado, duplex was really little more than a collection of boxy, low-ceilinged rooms that provided a stopover for sleeping and a place for storing equipment between runs. At first sight, homeowner and designer Sally Austen, owner of Sagebrush Design in Edwards, Colorado, was able to see a range of design possibilities. "I wasn't really in the market to buy," Sally recalled, "but I could see that the house had good bones. Although it was quite a challenge, I knew it could be exquisite."

Before she could consider the decorative elements, she had to open up the space and enlarge it. Sally began by turning the loggia that connected the house to the garage into a living room with a vaulted ceiling. She then turned a cramped 8-by-8-foot kitchen area into an L-shaped room that is pleasing to work in and great for entertaining. "I wanted to create a place where people could gather," she said.

The space that had originally been the living room became a casual area for dining and informal get-togethers, warmed by a big stone fireplace. For larger gatherings, Sally utilizes the foyer, which has a faux French refectory table that, with leaves, can open to 10 feet wide and seat eight.

Major work was needed to turn the dark, low-ceilinged hunter-green bedroom into a master suite. When removing the dark wood beams, Sally was happy to discover that the ceiling was false, and proceeded to open it

The Wish List

- Increase the home's interior living space from 2,500 to almost 3,800 square feet
- Add a formal living room, media room and study
- Create a vaulted ceiling so the loggia would become the living room
- Heighten the bedroom by removing crisscrossed beams and a false ceiling
- Widen the door area leading to the master bathroom
- Brighten and update all of the baths with marblelike ceramic or porcelain tiles
- Install a series of stacked windows on one side of the new living room to take greater advantage of the view

Introduction

When we ask the readers of the remodeling and decorating magazines we produce at Woman's Day Special Interest Publications to tell us what they'd like us to cover in our issues, one of their favorite topics is always before-and-after makeovers. These makeovers can take many forms, from giving a boring room a much-needed face-lift, to bumping out a wall to gain sorely needed space, to tackling a major whole-house renovation. Easy Home Makeovers covers this wide range of makeovers and is for anyone who is contemplating remodeling, updating, or simply refreshing their living space.

An essential remodeler's guidebook, Easy Home Makeovers showcases beautifully transformed kitchens, baths, bedrooms, living rooms, family rooms, basements, and even attics. Each makeover presented includes before-and-after photos, floor plans and detailed information on exactly what was done. In addition, tips and tricks from the pros, advice on how to find and work with a contractor, and step-by-step instructions on important remodeling techniques—from tiling to wallpapering—will see you successfully through the remodeling process.

Good luck with your remodeling endeavors! I know that Easy Home Makeovers will provide you with the ideas and inspiration you need to fill your home with your own personal style.

—Olivia Monjo,
Editor-in-Chief,
Woman's Day Special
Interest Publications

LEFT: By removing the ceiling beams, adding French doors and decorating in soft natural tones, designer Austen put the focus on the stone fireplace and opened the room up both literally and aesthetically. BELOW: At one time the living room, this cozy hearth room is now a place where informal get-togethers occur.

Before

Before

ABOVE: Once dark and dreary, the master bedroom had an 8-foot-high false ceiling that was beamed with dark wood. RIGHT: Now soaring to its full 15 feet, the new master bedroom is painted soothing seafoam green, creating a light and airy environment for the designer's spare, classically lined furniture.

ABOVE: The old master bath had unattractive maroon wallpaper and a dated flower-print border. LEFT: With its spacious new glassed-in shower and travertine countertop and floors, the completely renovated master bath has the look and feeling of a spa. OPPOSITE: A center of activity, the new, wide-open kitchen is larger and sports more cabinetry—both glass- and plain-fronted knotty hickory floors and an easy-to-move pine cabinet-workstation. Everything from appliances to tiles was selected not only for sophisticated good looks but also for easy maintenance. BELOW: The original kitchen had a confined, boxed-in feeling.

Before

up to its true height of 15 feet. Uncommon in the West, French doors were used in several rooms replacing the solid interior doors that gave the rooms a cramped feeling. She also had the worn carpeting throughout the house replaced with antique-looking hickory floors, and had all of the wall areas repainted in light tones to visually expand the rooms. Many of the windows were also replaced to bring in light and open the rooms to the natural beauty and year-round view outside.

Sally selected furniture with simple, clean lines, along with sisal and Oriental rugs, Jacobean pieces for fun, and informal arrangements of flowers. These items suit her desire to create a relaxing second home for her young family and extensive network of friends to enjoy.

Make the Most of Molding

The primary purpose of molding is to add interest to a room, and it need not always be installed horizontally.
• You can apply molding strips vertically to section off long walls and simulate paneling.
• You can create huge squares or rectangles framed in molding and, within these shapes, apply wallpaper or paint, or hang framed art.
• Keep in mind that crown molding has a profile that angles or steps outward. But cove molding always curves inward, so you can position it to help hide indirect lighting, which can give a soft, subtle glow to the upper portion of your walls.
• In a tall room furnished in a period style, you can apply a grid of cove molding to the ceiling to achieve a coffered effect.

Color Coated

New homeowners in Belvedere, California, an island facing an extension of the San Francisco Bay, fell in love with their home's spectacular water views and urged their interior designer, Linda Applewhite, of Linda Applewhite & Associates in nearby San Rafael, to minimize distractions. They requested walls and ceilings to be stark white to frame the views and create a backdrop for furnishings they wanted mainly in blue and green—their favorite colors. Applewhite obliged her clients, but tactfully warned them they might come to regret the absence of any warm colors.

Five years later, when the couple decided to remodel the kitchen, they called Applewhite and admitted their mistake. "The house never felt warm," said one of the homeowners. "It looked so cold and felt so cold, I hated going into the living room." On days when gray clouds hung low in the sky or fog

BELOW: Columns that frame the space between living and dining rooms were painted a shade more intense than the wall color. The owners' art and glass collections provide colorful accents. OPPOSITE, TOP: Soft Roman shades on living-room windows and French doors can be lowered when the sun pours in. The paint color in the room repeats the colors of the incredible water view seen through the windows. Twin sofas are upholstered in a lively stripe featuring the owners' favorite colors, blue and green. OPPOSITE, BOTTOM: Stunning views of Raccoon Straits and Angel Island are visible even at street level. Brick posts at the top of the front steps draw visitors to the entry from the concrete driveway where cars are parked.

The Wish List

- Add color by repainting walls and ceilings throughout the house, replacing the original cool blue-and-green color scheme with warm tones
- Redesign the kitchen so that it provides more space for cooking and dining, and flows easily into the family room
- Install window treatments where there had been none to control the impact of light from the bright California sun
- Reupholster existing furniture to reflect the new color palette and also complement the homeowners' art and glass collections
- Add decorative accents that pick up colors from existing rugs and accessories

shrouded the island, her clients' white walls looked drab, making the blue-and-green palette seem lifeless. The only real color was in the couple's collections of paintings and art glass displayed throughout the house. Applewhite was certain that adding rich colors to her clients' blue-and-green palette would soften the background for their collections and enhance their enjoyment of the bay, visible from nearly every window.

Their designer had no trouble convincing them to choose teal-green for living room walls, terra-cotta for the dining room, and pale apricot for the master bedroom and remodeled kitchen. And all the ceilings were repainted in a subtle yet fresh cream tone. With Applewhite's help, her clients selected new upholstery fabrics and new window treatments. "The house had no oomph," said one owner. "Now I walk through the door and think I'm really glad to be home."

ABOVE: The new palette was inspired by musical motifs painted on a custom armoire that holds the owners' music system. With teal-green and terra-cotta dominant, the piece creates a striking transition between the living and dining rooms. The homeowners started their collection of unusual walking sticks during one of their many visits to London.

ABOVE, RIGHT: An oblong table with a lacquered top is the dining room's centerpiece. Some of the owners' glass collection is displayed in the giant hutch. The rug inspired the colors chosen for the nubby seat covers of the pineapple-back chairs. RIGHT: Examples of the owners' art flank the door between the dining room and the family room-kitchen.

ABOVE: A cumbersome island and a breakfast bar crowded the inefficient kitchen. "You almost couldn't cook, and when you dined, all you could see were white cabinets," says one of the owners. RIGHT: A breakfast table and chairs occupy one end of the remodeled kitchen. Clear glass doors in the custom oak cabinetry denote the bar area. Counters are topped with granite.

ABOVE: A bright gold chenille duvet on the four-poster bed in the master bedroom punches up the pastel tone of the apricot-painted walls. The plaid curtains had been the room's only splash of color before the redecoration. LEFT: A three-panel screen, painted with Mother Goose motifs by the wife's great-grandmother, hangs on the wall behind a chaise in one corner of the bedroom.

Top Tip

"Color is personal, so I have to respect people's wishes," said designer Applewhite. "But I always warn them that it's going to be very cold living with blue and green. You must get some warmth in there! Most of us love and respond to warm colors."

Wield Color Power

How do you make rooms interesting when the architectural details are unimpressive, the furnishings are ho-hum and home-owners are reluctant to make changes?

New Canaan, Connecticut, designer Donna Gorman used color to create warmth, definition and excitement in what was once an all-white decor. She added a textured wallcovering to the living room and a vibrant combination of wallcoverings in the daughter's bedroom.

"The living room wallcovering adds the right amount of color without being oppressive," said Gorman. "In the other room we used multiple patterns because it's a more whimsical space."

Color and pattern are just what the doctor orders when you're feeling the malaise of neutrality. Designer Gorman has these suggestions to enliven a room with color:

- TAKE A RISK Color needs to be aggressive enough to make a statement in a room, whatever its size.
- MIX IT UP Multiple patterns create interest. Use coordinating wallpaper, as was done in the girl's bedroom, to add definition.
- WATCH THE BUDGET You can take more chances when things aren't too precious. The inexpensive bright yellow living room chairs make a statement without being treated as heirlooms.
- GET CRAFTY Have fun embellishing furniture and accessories with unusual details. The rickrack on the bed, pom-poms on the coverlet and trims on the pillows make this room unique.
- FOLLOW YOUR HEART When it comes to choosing colors, go with what makes you happy. Start with a rug or fabric pattern you love and build from there.

Size Preserved

Architect N. Lee Ligo, AIA, has worked on many large high-end projects over the years, but when it came to his own remodeling project, he preferred to stay small. Lee and his wife, Linda, purchased a modest beach house in Ponte Vedra Beach, Florida, where some homes are the size of ocean liners. Their house was originally a 1,550-square-foot bungalow, sheathed in dirty asbestos shingles and lost amid a tangle of tropical plants and trees. The Ligos were familiar with the property—they lived right across the street in a much grander house—but Lee insisted that "there was something about the place I liked." For years, he had walked past the open garage door, which revealed a rusty hulk of a car. "The day the title was transferred to us, the first thing I did was try to close the garage door, which immediately fell to the ground," he recalled.

Lee was intent on maintaining the diminutive scale and unpretentious feel of the Florida house, yet he also felt the need to perform a gut renovation. "The place hadn't been touched since it was built in 1949," he explained, "and interior walls were covered in nubby plywood that looked like cordovan shoe leather." By the time Lee was done, not one original interior wall was left standing. The living space was expanded without significantly altering the footprint of the house by building a bay window extension and enclosing a screened porch.

Before

TOP: What was once a screened-in porch became a comfortable enclosed winter garden. ABOVE: The original street elevation of the house, with overgrown greenery and worn asbestos shingles, can only be described as plain and dowdy.

Before

TOP: Architect Ligo remarked that he was "tired of yellow, white, and green in Florida houses." Instead, he chose soft caramel hues for the living-dining area to highlight the furnishings. ABOVE: The old living room was cramped and small, with knotty pine paneling and dark wood floors. RIGHT: The open doorway to the right of the fireplace in the living-dining area leads to the new winter garden.

ABOVE: The old house had paneling covering walls and ceilings. LEFT: This sunny guest bedroom features adjustable blinds that regulate light through the west-facing window, which is accented by a casually hung plaid-scarf valance. BELOW, LEFT AND RIGHT: Originally, the house's floor plan was a rabbit warren of spaces. Redesigned and modestly expanded, it became more open and felt more spacious. Even so, rooms remain distinct while melding with others. The windows, French doors, and winter garden let in fresh air and light.

The Wish List

- Add French doors to link the interior of the house more closely to outdoor areas
- Strip exterior walls of their worn quarter-inch plywood veneer
- Reconfigure interior spaces by removing walls to create more open, sunlit areas; paint remaining walls in light tones
- Install decorative woodwork in several rooms to create an illusion of height
- Replace one standard window with a bay window extension to visually widen the narrow living room
- Restore and repaint the garage, adding a new working door and antique architectural embellishments

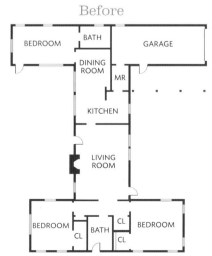

Before

After

Before

Improvising Cabinets

Lee is rarely able to let good building materials go unused. For the kitchen cabinets, he used several interior window shutters that date from the mid-19th century, which he discovered in an old Pennsylvania barn. He hired an Amish carpenter to turn them into modern-day cabinets.

- The shutters were stripped of varnish and white paint, then finished.
- Honey-maple surfaces were sprayed with a light shellac to create a slight sheen.
- Rather than deface the cabinets with hardware, Lee installed them to ensure that each opens easily by its corners.
- Kitchen drawers were also fashioned from shutters cut sideways.
- Lee designed the island counter on an angle as a way to maximize space.

Before

ABOVE: Before work began on the house, the front garden was a jungle of plants—an area that has since become an orderly outdoor room. LEFT: Lee built a glass-enclosed winter garden because of a lesson he learned: "You can't have a screened porch in Florida. Black soot invariably collects on the screens and coats the furniture."

The effect of the long, narrow living room, which Lee likened to a trailer, was mitigated by the addition of a rectangular bay window that makes a perfect dining alcove. The original fireplace remained, though it was redone with recycled bricks and enhanced with an art deco–style surround.

The use of salvaged materials and furnishings is a recurring theme in Lee's work. Here, a kitchen worktable from his grandmother's country house was refashioned into an elegant living room table. Except for some crown molding, most of the interior trims came from century-old Pennsylvania houses. Even the kitchen cabinets, made of window shutters, are recycled.

ABOVE: On a deck suspended over water, Lee placed and planted orange, tangerine, and kumquat trees. The pressure-treated wood deck requires virtually no maintenance.

The only really new living space is the "winter garden." Once a screened-in porch, it became an air-conditioned, year-round living area. In the winter garden, as elsewhere in the three-bedroom house, inexpensive, easy-to-maintain tile flooring was installed. Walkways and decks were created throughout the property to function as outdoor rooms surrounded by tropical plants and lush foliage native to the region. According to Lee, "This bungalow exemplifies my belief that the livability of a house is more important than its square footage."

ABOVE: The old garage door was always open to the elements. LEFT: Corbels from a circa-1870 Italianate house and slate roof tiles from a century-old barn adorn the renovated garage.

Salvaged Star

For years, Warner and Allison McConaughey longed to have a house of their own, but limited funds suggested that home ownership might be an impossible dream. Then Warner learned of a house auction in Atlanta, where they lived. "It was built in 1910, an American Foursquare," he says. "That was a really popular style after the Victorian period—a simple two-story home with simple rooms." It was also a mess, as it had been vacant for twenty years. In the 1960s, it had been converted into eight apartments, all of which shared a single bath. The roof was mostly missing, as were many of the windows.

Only one person was bidding against the McConaugheys; when he dropped out, they got the house for $15,900. Warner felt confident that given his and Allison's expertise—she is an interior designer; he is the founder and president of HammerSmith, a Decatur, Georgia, general contractor—they could bring the house back to something approaching its

TOP: The front porch was rebuilt around existing brick column bases. Pressure-treated pine flooring, railings and the beadboard ceiling are new; the wood columns were from a neighbor. ABOVE: Water damage was evident in the living room. OPPOSITE: The living room floor is the original heart pine, patched with pieces salvaged from the kitchen floor when that room was remodeled. The vintage light fixture is true to 1910 fashion.

ABOVE: A new roof, patched and repainted siding, plus a new front porch—supported by salvaged columns—restored this American Foursquare to its 1910 profile. RIGHT: The dilapidated house was acquired at auction.

DINING ROOM

KITCHEN

BATH

LIVING ROOM

ENTRY

FIRST FLOOR

SECOND FLOOR

MASTER
BATH

BEDROOM

MASTER
BEDROOM

DEN

With new windows added to the back of the house, the dining room now receives more sunlight than in the past. Most of the other improvements were either mechanical or cosmetic.

Once the warren of bedrooms was cleared out, the floor plan became more attuned to modern living, though still true to its Foursquare geometry and modest scale of the architecture.

former beauty. The two then embarked on a fifteen-year renovation, and it took a full year of initial spade work before they could even think of moving in. "The heating, cooling, electrical, and plumbing all had to be redone," Warner explained.

The couple was keen on restoring the house rather than redoing or updating it. The original exterior lap siding was in poor condition, but the McConaugheys patched rather than replaced what was no longer usable, salvaging siding off the back of the house, then scraping, sanding, and repainting each restored surface. The only exterior wall that was changed was the rear one, with new siding, new windows, French doors, and a two-story porch. "We moved some of the old windows off the back of the house and used them on the front and sides," said Warner.

Floors throughout the house are original heart pine. Wood bores and termites long ago softened some of the planks, but as new tile flooring was earmarked for the baths and kitchen, reusable planks were pulled up carefully from these spaces and put down in other parts of the house, then sanded and coated with protective polyurethane. During the course of restoring their home, which now has three bedrooms, Warner and Allison had two children—Zadie and Wilson. The couple's lives changed a lot during the years of restoration, but their vision for the house never wavered. "In remodeling or restoring a place, you have to have an overall plan for whatever you want to do," Warner declared. "Even if you're doing a piecemeal job, stopping and starting as we did, whenever you pick up again, you don't want to have to rework anything. The real secret is preplanning."

The Wish List

- Patch old siding and windows, and move reusable windows from the renovated rear exterior to where needed on the front and sides
- Install new roofing and build a new front porch supported by old columns bought from a neighbor
- Scrape, sand smooth, and paint all of the repaired exterior siding and trim
- Redo the rear exterior wall, adding new siding, windows, and French doors plus a new two-story porch
- Restore two fireplaces and repair the single brick chimney
- Patch and refinish the heart-pine floors, and put down new tile flooring in the baths and kitchen
- Use mostly salvaged materials to rebuild the front stairs, and create a new stairway access to the attic
- Convert the house's fourth bedroom into a new master bath, closet, and dressing room, and also redo the upstairs hall bathroom

OPPOSITE, TOP: Homeowner Warner McConaughey purchased the 1950s range for $100—five years before he had a kitchen to put it in. Now, placed against a wall of 5-by-8-inch ceramic tiles set in a bond pattern, it's the centerpiece. "The old hood above the range came from a job site," Warner said. "The owner didn't want it." OPPOSITE, BOTTOM: The front stairway is a mix of mostly old components: the heart-pine treads from a dealer in South Georgia, the posts from a local salvage store. The oak fireplace mantel was stripped, stained, and trimmed with tile saved from other fireplaces in the house. LEFT: The rear facade of the house was totally redone, with new windows and French doors behind a two-story porch that overlooks the new patio and landscaped yard.

Going Green

According to Bruce Drake, a professor at the University of Portland, Oregon, he has never been in a house he has liked more than this one. Bruce, who with his wife, Eileen, purchased this English Cottage-style dwelling in 2001, had spent weeks passing the "For Sale" sign in front of the house on his drive to work. "The house spoke to me," he said. "This wonderful blend of architectural styles, with the stone wall flowing almost organically into the house. It's very stately without being pretentious."

Although the 1928 house was virtually intact on the outside, "inside, it suffered from a bad case of the seventies," said Bruce, a revelation that was particularly disappointing since the house had been originally built by "The Oregonian" newspaper as a model home to show off local woods. The remodel during the 1970s looked dated and ugly—the previous owners had replaced an elegant set of French doors in the living room with a fixed pane of glass without muntins, installed dark-brown kitchen cabinets, and dropped the ceiling. They also used garish accents in an upstairs bath, and slathered so much paint on the wood staircase that the carved heads on the finials looked like abstract sculpture.

Not only did the Drakes want to restore the house, but they also "wanted to do so in a sustainable, environmentally friendly way," Bruce explained. The couple hired the Neil Kelly Company, a Portland-based firm known for its emphasis on environmentally conscious design.

ABOVE: The main staircase was stripped of paint and restored to its original wood finish. The custom-built bench was made from reclaimed fir. LEFT: The living room retained its original rustic charm. Walls were painted a soft maple; the stone fireplace and ceiling woodwork were cleaned professionally.

The Wish List

- Remove the front porch and reinstall a decorative lintel
- Replace a fixed window in the living room with French doors
- Install a new dining room window and build a window bench under it
- Create a cutting-edge kitchen after gutting the old one down to the original studs
- Create wall panels in the dining room with recycled wood
- Restore the main staircase by stripping off white paint, using nontoxic remover
- Remove a vanity to open up the second-floor bathroom

LEFT: The dining room walls were painted the color of straw, a slightly darker hue than in the living room. BELOW: When the Drakes bought the house the original paneling had been removed and new painted paneling installed.

Before

Before

ABOVE: The original wall panels in the library needed only a good cleaning. The room, now decorated with Arts and Crafts furnishings and reproductions of William Morris fabrics, retains its early-20th-century style. RIGHT: Project designer Richmond referred to the original woodwork in the library as being "pickled," a process that involved sandblasting the hemlock and fir panels to achieve a distressed texture. Four carved scenes, created shortly after the house was first built, depict life around Portland from the mid-1800s to the early 1900s. The window, with a fixed center panel and two casements, is new.

The project that Karen Richmond, a designer with Neil Kelly, and the Drakes undertook was recognized as an exemplar of "green" remodeling by Portland General Electric. The local utility created its Earth Advantage program to help people save energy and make responsible environmental choices during remodeling. At the Drake house, nontoxic paint remover was used to remove the thick finish on a staircase, and energy-efficient appliances were installed throughout the house.

Among the most dramatic aspects of the remodel was the replication of wainscoting in the dining room. Upon removing plasterboard, Drake discovered nail holes that revealed the dimensions and scale of the original wainscoting, which had been removed years earlier. In keeping with the green theme, the designer salvaged old fir-bleacher seats from a local high school and had them milled for the new period-style panels.

Richmond decided to take the kitchen down to the studs and replicate what had once been there. The new base cabinets she installed are fabricated from wheatboard, a formaldehyde-free substance derived from agricultural waste. Upper wall cabinets are made of mandrone, an environmentally sustainable red-hued Northwest wood.

ABOVE: In order to restore the home historically in an environmentally safe way it was necessary to gut the kitchen down to the studs and painstakingly replicate what had once been there. This meant each material and design decision had to be balanced between design, function, serviceability and price, and historic value and sustainability. Energy-saving appliances were used throughout.

ABOVE, RIGHT AND TOP: To improve the traffic flow in and out of an upstairs bathroom, a vanity, added in the 1970s, was removed. A pink-and-blue tub was replaced with a 1920s-style white porcelain model. Virtually all of the original tile in the bath was reusable. RIGHT: Before the renovation, the kitchen bore the dated image of dark cabinetry, fluorescent lighting and six layers of linoleum.

Classic Revival

At first glance, the small cape appears to be a typical New England clapboard farmhouse. Distinguished by a long, low-pitched roof that yields 3-foot, 8-inch second-floor side kneewalls and limited headroom, the house is picture-perfect in its rural Vermont setting. Since 1940, it has been owned by architect Pi Smith's family. First purchased by her grandparents, the property passed on to Smith's father, then to her. "A major renovation was definitely in order," she said. "The whole first-floor structure had rotted. There was no insulation, the windows leaked, and the heating system was poor. The house also had an unusual linear shape because a long, narrow L-shaped addition had been appended to the west gable end."

Smith's first step was to toss out the original floor plan of small rooms, multiple doorways, and limited traffic flow and rethink how to best use the total space via an open floor plan. Upstairs and down, walls were removed and repositioned, windows added, and rooms redesigned to create the illusion of a larger space. Attic space gave way to a child's playroom, a loft-style guest bedroom-lounge area, and a cathedral ceiling for the living room. The oversize entry hall was converted into a cozy dining room. A large guest bedroom was halved so a combo guest bath-laundry area could be added.

To further expand the space, dropped ceilings were removed, revealing one of the home's charming architectural features: original post-and-beam framing. Perhaps the biggest change of all was the stairway relocation and redesign. Now with a windowed landing and a view of the meadow, the switch-back staircase delivers traffic to the center of the second floor, making it possible to create a central hall and much-needed bath.

ABOVE: Recycled from the original building, the back barn door, although now just a decorative feature, is a charming part of the home's history. Skylights and new windows that flood the interior with daylight were added only on the back of the house so the front facade could remain as it had been for more than a century. OPPOSITE: An earthy palette adds warmth to white-painted walls. The cathedral ceilings and 4-foot half-wall were among the visual tricks Smith used to create the illusion of more space, enabling her to forgo adding square footage to the house.

Before

ABOVE: A beamed ceiling is the epitome of rustic atmosphere—but its flat, low plane contributed to the old interior's dark and claustrophobic feeling. LEFT: In the kitchen, angled spice racks built between original notched posts and an elongated cherry island provide additional work and dining spaces.

BELOW: A textbook example of making the most of a small space, the new master bath utilizes three walls for storage. Opposite kneewall cabinetry, the vanity has open shelving and closed cupboards. A shallow wraparound display shelf ties the look together.

ABOVE: What child wouldn't love such a whimsical bedroom? The soaring bead board ceiling and shutter-style window overlooking the loft and living room lend a tree house feel and let the imagination soar. The room's shape creates nooks and crannies that are ideal for hide-and-seek.
RIGHT: At the end of the L-shaped addition is the loft guest bedroom and lounge area. The space seems designed for adventuresome guests for whom scaling a ladder to reach a private nirvana is part of the fun of an overnight visit.

LEFT: Like other rooms in the house, the master bedroom was long on charm but short on storage, so a custom wainscot-style headboard was designed to incorporate overhead book and display shelves.

The Wish List

- Repair and preserve the front facade so it would still blend in with its traditional surroundings
- Add windows and skylights to fill the house with sunlight
- Create the illusion of greater interior space with an open floor plan and vaulted ceilings
- Knock down walls to eliminate small, boxy rooms and increase air circulation
- Relocate the staircase for a whole-house open floor plan and to make adding a second-floor bath possible
- Reconfigure rooms to fit the family's lifestyle
- Increase the house's overall storage capacity

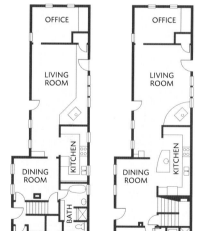

FIRST FLOOR

BEFORE

AFTER

SECOND FLOOR

BEFORE

AFTER

BEFORE: Originally a choppy, congested space, the old ground level of the farmhouse was ill suited to modern living. AFTER: Removing the wall between kitchen and dining room increased both space and light. The floor plan was further streamlined by relocating and reconfiguring the staircase.

BEFORE: The existing second floor lacked a critical modern convenience: there was no bathroom to service the two bedrooms. AFTER: Upstairs, the effects of shifting the staircase—which now includes a landing—were dramatic, providing more than enough space for the desired master bath.

Bungalow Update

"When I first saw the house, I felt it was something I'd love to work on and make into a home," says Jim Blasi. His partner, Michael Tozzoli, had just the opposite reaction: "I felt overwhelmed—it needed so much work." But Blasi prevailed, and the two-story house became theirs.

Luckily, the previous owner had made few improvements. "In some ways, that was a plus," Michael believes. "She hadn't put walls where they didn't belong and mainly hadn't wrecked it." The house, which dates from the 1920s, is a classic bungalow. Aware of its origins, Jim did some research and found that bungalows of that vintage usually had covered front porches. Instead, this one had an enclosed sunroom. Removing the windows and glass door, the siding and interior panels, the owners discovered a fairly intact front porch that mainly needed coats of paint.

But most of all, the house would need to grow. Set at the front of a 50-by-150-foot lot, it could only be expanded to the rear, and since both floors would be involved, it was clear that professional help was needed. Enter Xiomara C. Paredes, AIA, and Glenn A. Grube, RA, of Paredes-Grube Architecture in Glen Rock, New Jersey.

ABOVE: All of the exterior was replaced by new siding and stucco was applied more than halfway up the two-story walls. The front porch, now open and airy, had been enclosed prior to the renovation. BELOW: A new back porch was notched into the 660-square-foot rear addition. BOTTOM: Originally, the back of the house had a shedlike roof over utilitarian steps. Adding personality here was a priority for the homeowners.

Before

LEFT: The owners designed the raised fireplace, which is the centerpiece of the new family room. The handcrafted mantel and tile treatment are appropriate to a vintage bungalow. OPPOSITE: Triple windows bring daylight and a view of the backyard into the new family room. Recessed ceiling lights and an antique bronze chandelier make this room literally glow at night.

LEFT: Two square columns and the tile floor create an illusion of separation for the breakfast area. The window became a focal point, thanks to the colorful window treatment; wood blinds from a home center provide privacy. BELOW: Its walls lightened, and now illuminated by a trio of deeply suspended lanterns, the refurnished dining room was merely tweaked during the six-month remodel. BOTTOM: The old dining table and chairs, as well as the imitation Tiffany light fixture, were replaced, as they suggested a style no longer appropriate to the homeowners' view of the house.

FIRST FLOOR The house was expanded rearward to create a back porch and a more attractive facade. Inside, the old powder room became a full bath.

SECOND FLOOR One small bedroom and part of the new addition became the master suite, which contains its own comfortable sitting area.

Before

Before

ABOVE: Before the renovation, the kitchen was cramped and dated. Reworking the space was crucial, as the owners spend a lot of time there. RIGHT: Mollie, the family pet, knows her place in the reordered kitchen. Granite counters sweep the length of the wall where the range is placed, then angle off into a two-tiered L. The raised portion adds bonus storage on both sides and also shields the cook and mess from anyone who happens to be sitting in the adjacent breakfast room.

The Wish List

- Create a two-story rear extension that would include a back porch, family room, breakfast room, expanded kitchen, and master bedroom
- Improve the exterior by applying stucco and siding plus new asphalt-tile roofing
- Add new landscaping and a tiny backyard fish pond
- Repair interior wood trim and add grandeur with Arts and Crafts-style columns
- Install new hardwood flooring throughout the house
- Uncover the front porch and dining room fireplace, both of which had been hidden for more than twenty years
- Expand the first-floor bedroom and turn the powder room into a full bath

The architects went to work designing a 660-square-foot extension: On the main floor, they added a family room, and expanded a bedroom and the kitchen to include a breakfast area; on the second floor, they created a spacious new master bedroom. They also notched out a gracious back porch, with railings that mimicked those at the front of the house.

"The house has enough details to be categorized an Arts and Crafts structure," says Paredes, "so the clients' first goal was to emphasize those aspects." In the kitchen and family room, wall and pendant fixtures reflecting the style were installed, and period wood trim throughout the house was repaired and freshened. As would have been done in Arts and Crafts–style homes of the early 20th century, two square columns were installed in the new wing to make the breakfast area feel separate.

Jim and Michael, who like to cook and entertain, knew that even with a new addition, kitchen space would be limited, so they sought help from kitchen designer Ned Spenadel, of Home Supply & Lumber Center in Hawthorne, New Jersey. He designed the custom cherry cabinets and bilevel peninsula. A downstairs bedroom, once used as a den, became a guest room, and the powder room was torn out and doubled in size to become a full bath. Upstairs, one bedroom and part of the new addition morphed into a 12-by-34-foot master suite, with views overlooking the backyard garden and pond.

New white oak flooring throughout, except for the tiled rooms, knit new and old spaces together seamlessly. "Everything looks as though it was always there," said Grube. "And that's just what the owners intended."

TOP: A tiny first-floor bedroom, which the owners had used as a den, was expanded to become a full-size guest room. The door, unchanged from the original plan, opens into the living room. ABOVE: The sleeping area of the expanded master suite is centered between two angled roof beams. Windows on three sides flood the room with light. RIGHT: The guest bath, with its frameless glass shower, is more than twice the size of the previous powder room. Topped with granite and an undermount sink, the vanity is a custom designed unit.

Before

ABOVE: The diminutive single-story house featured an asphalt-shingled roof, plain board-and-batten cladding, and one front window that was fixed in the center with casements on either side. LEFT: Visible from the street is a soaring wall of windows contained in an arcing structure supported by bow-string trusses. A Dutch-style front door is covered with a copper overhang that matches the roofing. BELOW: In the living-dining area, the lower windows are operable; the rest are fixed. Track lights are tucked into center cavities in the trusses, which owner-architect Jones had sandblasted for texture. Mortarless cultured stones, also used on the exterior, form the chimney. The Douglas fir mantel is substantial, in keeping with the dramatic scale of the room.

Opened to Light

In the midst of a dramatic remodeling project, Steve and Stephanie Jones's then four-year-old son, Quinn, called their home "The Fix-It House." Despite the fact that the job required the elimination of all but one wall, the Joneses continued to live in their Manhattan Beach, California, house. According to Steve, an architect who created the new design, "Quinn got to see how a house gets built. When he turned six, he talked about wanting to be an architect."

For two years, the Joneses had lived in a one-story house in the Tree Section, one of three neighborhoods in Manhattan Beach, named for its many trees. The house was small and dated, yet Steve could see that it had a great deal of potential. It wasn't until Stephanie became pregnant with their second child that the couple decided to embark on a remodel that would take more than eight months and add 1,910 square feet of living space to the house. The project included expanding the footprint, adding three stories and transforming the single-car garage to a two-car space.

The first evidence of the house's transformation is revealed by the living-dining area. "My biggest goal was to open the house to light and make it feel larger," Steve explained. To bring in the California sun, he fashioned a soaring 21-foot-high room with an arcing ceiling supported by conspicuous bow-string trusses. Walls of windows took the place of solid drywall. A roughly textured stone fireplace became a new visual anchor.

By taking advantage of unused land on the sloping property, Steve was able to expand the house and create an open kitchen-family room in the rear, an area also defined by the fireplace. In classic California tradition, the design allows outdoor areas to meld with the indoors—via oversize sliding doors that lead to a deck.

To make the transition from indoors to outdoors virtually seamless, a redwood deck was built exactly on level with the family room floor.

Top Tip

In any interior redo, be sure sight lines are good—especially if your household includes young children. In a kitchen, place appliances, sinks, and eating areas so broad stretches of rooms and outdoor areas are plainly visible.

LEFT: Paduk, an African wood, was used for the kitchen cabinets. Over time, it darkens from brilliant orange to nut-brown. Wall cabinet doors have rice paper inserted between layers of glass for added texture. BELOW: The oversize kitchen island holds storage drawers plus two pullout chrome wire racks—one for fruit, the other for vegetables.

Although the house appears taller than before, Steve adhered to the city's 26-foot height restriction by stacking the house as a series of split-levels: beginning with the garage, followed by the main living areas, then a mid-level bedroom-office suite, and finally an upstairs with three bedrooms. The view from each of them is eye level with the neighborhood's pepper trees—not unlike being in a tree house, albeit an extremely luxurious one.

ABOVE: In the family room, Steve allowed for a spacious 16-inch-high fireplace ledge, where his children could play board games. The fireplace wraps the corner so that it can be enjoyed from the deck.

The Wish List

- Add 1,910 square feet and three stories
- Erect an outdoor deck that is absolutely level with the interior floor of the family room
- Replace the single-car garage with a two-car space in compliance with local building codes
- Design and build a combination guest bedroom and office suite over the new garage
- Finish the facade, interior chimney, and hearth using mortarless cultured stone
- Create an open floor plan for the first floor
- Build floor-to-ceiling window walls on the front of the house with both operable and fixed frames
- Design and install a new, extra-large kitchen with a center island accessible to all appliances

ABOVE: The vanity in the master bathroom is topped with a synthetic translucent material in a soothing green. A 2-inch strip of mirror film was sand-blasted to create a frosted-glass look; behind it, a cathode tube supplies light. LEFT: Sliding windows in the master bedroom offer a view of the treetops. A mahogany ceiling fan keeps the room cool in California's warm summers.

ABOVE: The 16-by-20-foot redwood deck is on the same level as the family room floor, creating a seamless effect between indoors and out. Steve used 20-foot sections of wood to avoid joint lines.

OPEN TO BELOW

Before   After—LOWER LEVEL   After—UPPER LEVEL

FAR LEFT: The original house had 840 square feet of living space. Although building codes allowed using up to 3,100 square feet of land, Steve decided to expand upward to preserve existing trees on the property. CENTER, LEFT: To adhere to a city code requiring a two-car garage, Steve fashioned a tandem one. The footprint was extended 5 feet on the south side and 23 feet on the west. Downstairs living zones include a living-dining area and a family room-kitchen. LEFT: A mid-level guest bedroom-office is positioned above the garage. A fourth level contains the three main bedrooms. The remodeled house's square footage is 2,750 feet.

Fabulous Finishes

Plain white walls are blank canvases full of possibilities. Instead of decorating them with wallpaper or pictures, why not paint your own one-of-a-kind finish? Three techniques—color washing, ragging, and sponging—are perfect for beginners. All produce quite different results: color washing creates the delicate look of watercolor; ragging offers soft texture; sponging has a marbled effect.

Be sure you practice on objects other than the intended surface to help you master these methods.

EMULATE THE PROS

Know what products will and won't do—and buy materials the professionals choose. Favor Polyvine, a water-based glaze that stays wet three times longer than other manufactured glazes. Buy 2-inch-wide low-tack tape. Professional painters use it to tape off ceilings because, when peeled off, it won't take half the surface with it.

Prepare, prepare, prepare. As tedious as it sounds, hours spent in preparation will yield a better-than-expected result. That means: tape off sidewalls, ceilings, and baseboards; clean and wash surfaces, and get rid of loose paint chips; fill and sand holes and cracks; lay drop cloths to protect furniture, rugs, and collectibles.

THINK 45 DEGREES

The angle at which paint is applied can determine the difference between noticeable lap lines and a well-blended surface. Painting horizontally and vertically, unless glazes are immediately worked in, can result in unwanted stripes. Instead, pros recommend using the 45-degree method, brushing or ragging or sponging on an angle.

PICK THE POSITIVE

It is easier to add paint than to subtract it. Known as positive techniques, color washing, ragging, and sponging share a common methodology. Translucent glaze is piled atop a base coat by one person using brushes, sponges, or rags. Conversely, a negative technique requires two people—one to apply, the other to remove.

SAMPLE IT

An hour or so experimenting with colors and finishes on 20-by-20-inch poster boards will save days of work. Why not pick a tone on tone—one shade slightly darker than the first—and try your hand.

Italians named these faux finishes well, calling them *arte povera*, or poor man's art.

TOP: Use a colorwash for a more weathered look. It's also a good choice to hide imperfections in walls. ABOVE, CENTER: Ragging is the recommended technique for beginners. Glazes were applied to this wall with a ragging mitt. ABOVE: Decorative paint techniques, like sponging enliven the look of any room.

With the ever-increasing popularity of decorative painting, more manufacturers now offer all-in-one "high-styled" packages of supplies. Experts opt for the best and most effective materials, as directed by the technique. Their recommendations:

- BRUSHES Color washing needs only the cheapest synthetic tools, since this process permanently damages a brush's bristles; ragging deserves a 2½-inch angle brush for glazing to get into the edges and corners.
- GLAZES Forget mixing any yourself. Buy premade products, preferably water based, that will allow for some drying time.
- PAINTS Oil-based versus water-based? No contest: water-based paints are the way to go. The smell of oils alone will drive you crazy, not to mention that oils yellow over time.
- RAGS Many specialty stores sell bags of clean T-shirts. The price is well worth the time it takes to wash, dry, and remove lint from household cloths.
- SAFETY FIRST Got respiratory problems? Even if materials are water based, mask up and wear gloves.
- SPONGES Buy the natural marine kind, not cellulose. For $35, you can get a large one, but rinse it out after every use.
- TAPE, DROP CLOTHS AND ALL-PURPOSE COVER-UPS Remember: protection and preparation are key. Use low-tack tape, and wear clothes that wash easily and well.

IN DETAILS: RAGGING TECHNIQUE

While the most popular paint technique is sponging, ragging is the easiest technique for anyone to master.

Tools and materials

- blue painter's tape, buckets (for water and clean-up)
- gloves
- lint-free rags (or old T-shirts)
- paint roller and cover
- paint tray, plastic liner, plastic tray liner
- paper towels
- two tones of interior latex satin paint

NOTE: Use a premade glaze and tint it with one tone of the paint, mixing in a few paint drops at a time to achieve a four-to-one ratio and a translucent quality.

1 Before applying the first coat, make sure that walls are clean and free of holes. Use an interior latex satin paint as your base coat. Once it dries, mask off the trim, the ceiling, and the baseboards with blue painter's tape.

2 Gather the rags and cut them into large pieces that can be bunched up but still nestle comfortably in your hand.

3 To apply the glaze, line your paint tray with a plastic liner. Pour a small amount of paint into the tray. Keep paper towels handy to dab off any unwanted paint during the glazing process.

4 Practice makes perfect. Dampen the rag to remove any remaining lint, then wring it out well. Bunch it into random folds—the fewer flat areas, the better. Dip it into the top-coat color, blotting off excess on the liner and then on paper towels.

5 Start on a wall. Begin at a center point, gently pressing the rag to leave an impression. Work on a 45-degree angle in a space about 2 feet square. Since the first impressions will be heavier, space them out a bit and fill in the spaces between the heavier spots for a soft blending effect. When you rag, rotate your wrist to vary the pattern. Bunch the rag periodically to create different textures and shapes.

6 Rinse the rag often for a crisp crushed design. Work your way around the room, in 45-degree-angle puzzle shapes, until the job is done.

ABOVE: Ragging with a rich hue has transformed this bedroom into an elegant retreat.

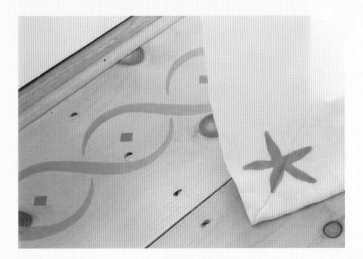

Painted border

Stenciling a simple repeating pattern will dramatically change the look of a room and establish a theme that can be echoed in decorative accessories. Paint the floor with earth tones to complement wood; for a bolder statement, try a bright blue.

For best results, start with a new floor or one that's been sanded to the bare wood. For faded or stained hardwood floors, consider painting the floor prior to stenciling with two coats of a solid color paint. Or create an impressive "inlaid" border by using wood stain in lieu of paint: apply an overall wood stain in a lighter color, then block out a border design with painter's tape and blot on a darker wood stain with a rag. To seal and protect any creation, apply several coats of polyurethane or varnish.

Ranch Revival

When Mark McIntire and Stuart Sklar bought their vacation home within walking distance of the village of Southampton, New York, a seaside area of Long Island, they were attracted to its simplicity and workable space. "We knew we could easily make it comfortable," said Stuart.

Built in 1963, the modest ranch-style house was one of four similar small-scale structures that had once been home to families working the fields of an adjacent potato farm. That farm, long gone, was ultimately turned into a residential development. High hedges now shield Mark and Stuart's house from neighbors beyond its half-acre site.

"For us, part of its appeal was that, though small, this was a one-level house," Mark explained. Originally, it had two bedrooms and one bath, but a previous owner had added a lean-to structure containing a second bath, attached like a barnacle to the rear of the house.

When they sat down to plan the renovation, Mark and Stuart decided to expand living spaces and create three state-of-the-art bathrooms, a sizable master bedroom, plus a new kitchen sized and equipped for entertaining. Even with such ambitious goals, said Mark, "We wanted the house to look as though it had always been that way." They turned to architect Darren J. Helgesen, AIA, in Amagansett, New York, and his builder of choice, the late James Spooner, of James E. Spooner Construction in nearby Bridgehampton. The team worked on the inside and outside of the house—replacing plumbing, appliances, flooring, and wood trim as well as siding, roofing, some parts of the roof structure, and windows.

Initially, Mark and Stuart feared that adding a second story was the only

Before

ABOVE: Before the renovation, the living room was arranged around a painted brick fireplace set between built-in shelving and cupboards. The ceiling, which flowed into the dining room, was flat. OPPOSITE: To give the living room more character, architect Helgesen raised the roof and designed a cathedral ceiling, setting the space apart. The fireplace wall was redesigned; the shelves on either side hold some of Stuart's pottery collection.

BELOW, LEFT: Large new windows let natural light pour into the living room. Wood paneling, layers of molding, and a marble surround deftly obscure the home's original brick fireplace. BELOW, RIGHT: The dining room faces sliders that open out to the pool deck and pergola. Furnishings here and throughout the house were obtained from auctions and over the Internet, plus thoughtful friends and family.

ABOVE: The living and dining rooms flow together as one continuous space. The only separation was underscored by the cathedral ceiling and the arrangement of furnishings. BELOW: Expanded and repositioned, the new kitchen is 16 feet long with an easily maintained slate floor. Beneath the microwave is a two-door pantry with roll-out shelving.

ABOVE: A bow-shaped breakfast bar rises 4 inches above the level of the granite-topped work space that flanks the kitchen's large stainless steel undermount sink. BELOW: Except for the granite-topped breakfast bar, which rises a few inches above the counter, the kitchen is open to the adjacent dining room. The colorful backsplash is glass tile.

way for them to have the new master suite they coveted. They were delighted and felt reassured when Helgesen said it made more sense and was a lot less expensive to expand outward. "We did move a lot of things around," Helgesen recalled, "like extending the back of the house by 8 feet so we could increase the size of the kitchen, dining and guest rooms."

Most important, a wing was added to each end of the house. One replaced the old single-car garage with a two-car version, behind which were three storage bays; the other wing contained a new master bedroom, a bathroom, and a private outdoor deck. What had been 1,650 square feet, including the attached garage, was expanded to just over 2,500 square feet.

"We wanted the house to be focused on the backyard, where previous owners had installed a pool," said Mark. "So Darren not only added new windows but replaced all the others with larger ones." Outside, a new pergola, placed behind the garage, defines a gracious entertaining area only a few steps from the kitchen. A 5-foot band of new mahogany decking, built low to the ground, frames the pool.

Despite changes that widened the footprint substantially, Mark and Stuart were relieved that the house maintained its original character yet had a seamless transition to the backyard. The redesign makes the most of available space indoors and out. It has become a sunny, airy house that feels quite spacious, with exterior spaces ideal for seasonal entertaining. "Our house is laid out very comfortably," said Mark. "Now, when we have guests, our friends can come and go freely without interrupting the cook."

ABOVE: Natural quartz tops the tub deck and counter in the new master bath. Flooring is marble; wainscoting and backsplash are sparkling glass tile.

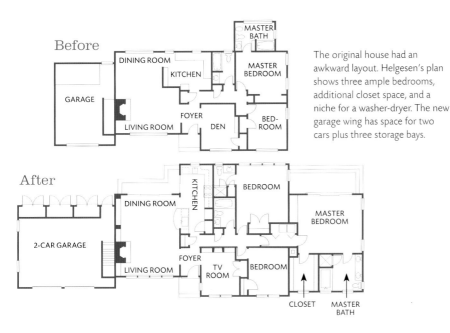

The original house had an awkward layout. Helgesen's plan shows three ample bedrooms, additional closet space, and a niche for a washer-dryer. The new garage wing has space for two cars plus three storage bays.

The Wish List

- Expand the original house to include a new kitchen, master suite, and two-car garage
- Apply new cedar shingles to the roof and exterior walls
- Create three new baths
- Replace the old floors with new white oak flooring
- Install a pergola and build a new patio
- Add a new mahogany deck to frame the pool

Before

Creating a Warm Welcome

Problem The dark entrance to this sixteen-year-old home was hardly what owner and designer Lisa Worth would call welcoming. The owner of Worth Interior Design in Aurora, Ontario, she bought the house in 2001. At the time, she recalled, "There was nothing that caught your eye in terms of the molding or color. Everything was drab and old." The ceramic floor tiles had a sheen that accentuated the tiniest amount of dust. A single small ceiling fixture with a 60-watt bulb barely illuminated the 280-square-foot space. Narrow 3-inch baseboards were out of proportion with the foyer's large scale, the stair carpet was worn, and the walls were a bleak light gray.

Solution To add more warmth and texture to the space, Lisa replaced the old gray floor tiles with mocha-colored Italian travertine whose varied pattern completely camouflages dirt. She also covered the stairs with a warm oatmeal-colored wool-and-synthetic carpet that's much more durable than the original silver-gray nylon rug.

Lisa designed 55-inch-high paneling both for the foyer and the staircase wall to add visual height. Painting the banister spindles white tied the staircase visually to the rest of the area. To brighten the foyer, she had five halogen spotlights installed around the perimeter, highlighting the wainscoting plus all the art on the walls.

TOP: Not even a curved staircase could make the old foyer inviting or interesting. ABOVE AND ABOVE, LEFT: Designer Worth brightened her foyer with new stair carpeting, a travertine floor, and white wood paneling.

DECORATIVE PANELING

Applying wainscoting is one of the easiest ways to perk up a room. The term refers to the decorative paneling or planking and trim attached to a wall, extending from the floor to either chair-rail height (36 inches) or plate-rail height (48 to 60 inches). Bead board (individual tongue-and-groove boards) is commonly used to create wainscoting and is available at home centers and lumberyards.

Tools and materials

- bead board panels
- wainscoting ply cap
- finishing nails (6-penny or 8- penny)
- construction adhesive
- wood filler
- primer and paint or stain
- pry bar
- stud finder
- tape measure
- 4-foot level
- power saw
- hammer
- jigsaw
- safety glasses
- notched trowel

1 Pry the baseboard from the wall, taking care not to damage it. Turn off the electric power and install box extension rings around all wall outlets. These metal collars will allow each outlet to be brought to the wainscoting's surface.

2 Decide how high your wainscoting should be. Measure up from the floor and, with a level, extend a line around the room or those wall segments you want to cover. Use a stud finder to locate the studs that will hold the cap rail and the baseboard.

3 Wearing safety glasses, cut the first section of paneling to the height between the floor and the level line, using a heavy-duty circular saw, an easy-handling 4- to 5-inch trim saw or a combination multitool depending on the paneling's thickness.

4 Mark the position of the electrical outlets and use a jigsaw to cut out appropriate rectangles in the bead board. Run a line of construction adhesive along the back of the board and spread it with a notched trowel. Place the board into a corner and nail into place, pressing along the board to help it bond.

5 Continue cutting and applying panels, nailing where studs are marked. The panels have a lip at the edges to hide the seams, but if the wainscoting is due for painting, apply a bead of paintable latex caulk for a smoother finish. Apply caulk in the corners as well.

6 Measure, cut, and nail the ply cap in place with 6- or 8-penny nails (they should reach about a half-inch into the studs). Miter the inside and outside corners. Reattach the baseboard with 8-penny nails, also mitering the corners. Countersink the nails, then fill all nail holes or seal any gaps with white latex caulk.

Bedroom

Heidi and Eric Brooks had lived in their Santa Monica, California, cottage for two years until they decided to upgrade the master bedroom. Before moving in, the couple had selected wall paint to use throughout the house and pulled up old shag carpeting to reveal oak floors. Later, they hung elegant curtains in their bedroom. "They were a gift from a friend," said Sasha Emerson, of Sasha Emerson Design in Santa Monica, who spent two months helping the couple play up their bedroom without beating up their budget.

The room was long and relatively narrow: about 15 by 30 feet. The bed was at one end and a TV and computer sat on tables at the other end. "Heidi called one day," Emerson recalled. "She said, 'All I have is a nice bed with a comfortable mattress and nice curtains. I want our bedroom to have a sitting area that's pretty to look at but still leaves room for a desk.'"

Heidi envisioned an English-style sitting room, which gave Sasha her cue: flea markets and thrift shops. "One of the niceties of English country is that you can mix high and low," she reported. "For instance, the sofa and armchair came from a low-budget antiques store. I had both pieces redone in six-dollar-a-yard fabric. I designed the ottoman and had it made—down to the chocolate-brown-stained legs. The fabric came from flea-market curtain panels, and some of it was used to cover a pillow on the armchair."

The bed was fairly new, but Emerson designed a headboard upholstered in an oyster-colored linen and covered the throw pillows with mostly vintage fabrics. "Those panels above the sofa came from an English folding screen at a flea market," Emerson recalled. "We divided it in three and hung it as art." On other walls are images Sasha unearthed in her flea market visits and reframed. "You can do English country on a budget," she said.

ABOVE: Heidi and Eric's bare bed dominated one part of the master bedroom. With no window treatment and no accessories on the bed, the room felt empty and, said Heidi, at times claustrophobic. BELOW, LEFT: The area opposite the bed is now furnished as a comfortable English-style sitting room, with thrift shop purchases augmented by an ottoman that designer Emerson created for the couple and had custom made and upholstered.

What They Loved

- The scale of the room. "It was big, but we didn't know what to do with it," recalled Heidi.
- The ocean breezes and natural light pouring in through the windows. "I loved that the windows faced west, toward the Pacific," she said.
- The pristine quality of the hardwood floor. According to Heidi, "We applied a chocolate stain to give it a more substantial look."

What They Hated

- The room's bowling-alley feel: a long, narrow space that lacked creative attention.
- The dichotomy of a nifty bed at one end, ratty furniture at the other.
- There was no place to sit and relax, and no area for the children to congregate.

ABOVE: The thrift shop desk and chair fit neatly on one side of the sitting area. The desk lamp was a cloisonné vase that designer Emerson made into a lamp, adding a newly recovered shade. LEFT: She found the antique trunk at a flea market and had it refinished before placing it at the end of the bed. The same linen that covers the upholstered headboard was used to create a bed skirt.

BELOW, LEFT: The base of this bedside lamp was once a vase. Beside it is the original bed, with a newly slipcovered and upholstered headboard. BELOW, CENTER: Pale blue welting on the reupholstered thrift shop armchair picks up tones in the sofa and ottoman. The elegant linen curtains, which the homeowners received as a gift, would have cost as much as all the rest of the furnishings.

BELOW, RIGHT: Before work was done, assorted tables and storage gear were clustered at one end of the bedroom. Heidi wanted a desk for her computer; she also wanted a comfortable space to sit, in effect, an upstairs family room.

Before

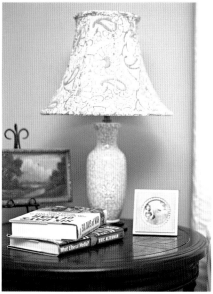

Family Room

After spending their first sixteen years of marriage in a tiny starter home, Jaimie and John LaMarca finally moved to a larger house—a two-story colonial in Glen Head, New York, that was built in 1913. "Back in the 1970s," says Jaimie, "the house was expanded to include a new garage, a guest room, and a guest bath, plus the extra-large room we now call the family room."

With two daughters, Emily, twelve, and Nicole, sixteen, the LaMarcas thought it was great having a 15-by-20-foot family room where everyone could gather. The problem was they didn't really know what to do with the space. "It had an ugly stained carpet and vertical blinds that didn't match the character of the house at all," Jaimie recalled. "I put a couple of old chairs, the TV, and the dog's bed in there, but it was never a comfortable place for us to hang out."

After letting the space languish for more than a year, Jaimie knew it was time to make it a room the family would actually use and enjoy. But wanting to furnish it affordably, she first enlisted family and friends to help her create the space she desired. After pulling up the ratty old carpeting, Jaimie recalled, "We found red oak flooring underneath and immediately had it refinished." Finally, she was ready to decorate.

Enter Jean Nayar, editor of "Budget Decorating" magazine. Working with Jaimie, over the course of a few months, Jean helped Jaimie reuse some of her existing furnishings, select some new ones, and choose fabrics

Before

ABOVE: Before work was done, two inherited side chairs flanked the wooden mini dry sink in the only part of the family room that was at least minimally furnished. BELOW: The old dog bed and a few pieces of otherwise homeless furniture were randomly placed within the existing room.

Before

ABOVE: Beneath the lift-off pitted-glass top of the "keepsake table," which is a new piece finished to look old, are porcelain boxes that Jaimie collects. The lower shelf holds part of her collection of Shaker stack boxes and painted wood candle holders. LEFT: In the spruced-up family room, an adjustable Roman shade provides privacy and shields light from the front-facing window. A new floral fabric skirts a round table that Jaimie inherited from one of her grandmothers.

ABOVE: Double doors that close off the computer armoire open flat, out of the way, when the unit is in use. The side chair upholstered in leatherette is one of a pair that came from Jaimie's dad's office. RIGHT: The new computer armoire has turned one corner of the room into a work area. Hanging from its handles is a plaque with a cut-out heart and stars, a gift from Jaimie's sister. The club chair and ottoman are covered in a delicate-looking but family-friendly, stain-resistant micro-suede.

What They Loved
- The size of the room
- The room's location just off the dining area, where it can easily serve as the central hub of the house
- The large windows, one of which looks out on trees beyond the deck

What They Hated
- The existing carpeting
- The old, ugly vertical blinds on the windows
- A lack of visual warmth
- The room was so sparsely furnished that it went mostly unused

and paint colors that complemented the palette of a rug—a gift from a family member—that now covers the floor. New window treatments that would add color and control light were also at the top of Jaimie's wish list. So Jean designed some simple Roman shades, which a friend helped to fabricate and Jaimie's husband, John, helped to install.

The LaMarcas wanted the room to be multipurpose, so that it would be possible for anyone watching TV to coexist with someone reading or using the computer. So, on one side of the long room, a new coffee table, an upholstered sofa, a love seat, a chair, and ottomans were arranged to face a new console that holds the TV, DVDs, and videotapes. On the other side of the space, a new computer armoire serves as a self-contained home office, and an existing wooden chest was topped with a box cushion and converted into a functional semblance of the window seat Jaimie had always wanted. Finally, new cushions and a pretty fabric topper over a recycled side table complement the shades and bring finishing touches to the room.

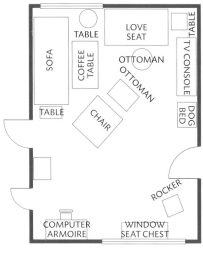

ABOVE: A love seat with throw pillows dominates the TV area. The wicker footstool also serves as a seat or a table. The lamp and table in the corner had once belonged to Jaimie's mother. FAR LEFT: The new floor plan shows how the LaMarcas' family room was divided into zones for reading, watching TV, and socializing. LEFT: An antique miniature dry sink, which the LaMarcas bought as newlyweds, now has a place of honor by the wall between the guest bath on the left and the guest room on the right. The round, gilded mirror and ceramic pitcher were recent purchases to accent the dry sink.

How to Pick a Wallpaper

Whether you opt for a showy floral or mod geometric will, of course, depend on your taste and the style of your home. But also factor in the room's exposure. If it's a sunny space, remember that the color of your paper will be intensified. If the particular room gets little natural light, a bright, cheery paper can give it life. Whatever pattern you choose, it's sure to add character and richness to your home that plain painted walls simply can't. Here are four stunning examples.

1. ACCENTUATE A WALL

Instead of papering an entire room, paper just one wall to create a unique look. In a dining room, the wall behind a sideboard is a good option. In a bathroom, try the mirror wall. The logical spot for wallpaper in a bedroom is the wall directly behind the bed, as shown.

2. CREATE AN AESTHETIC FOCAL POINT

Scrap cuttings of scenic papers (landscape, hunting, historic) can be used to create a handsome—and expensive-looking—mural when framed in picture molding and centered on a wall.

3. FORGE A MORE BECKONING ENTRY

Even a tiny entry or modest-size foyer can be visually expanded with wallpaper that adds intrigue and depth. As shown here, a pattern striped in beguiling bamboo trees also lifts the eye, making a small space seem much grander.

4. MAKE A ROOM SHINE

A metallic wallpaper can bring more reflective light into a dark room. Here, a gold leaf motif catches sun by day and subtly reflects the glow of a chandelier at night.

PAPER WORK

Offering more than just decorative appeal, wallpaper can change the perception of a room's size, scale, and feel. Bold patterns and rich colors can transform an airy space into a cozy lair, while light tones and subtle designs can make a small room appear much larger. Plus, wallpaper is often more visually engaging than a coat of paint. For a major style upgrade, this 12-by-14-foot bedroom was enhanced with whimsical paper in restful shades of green. The steps taken can work for almost any papering project. Here's how it was done.

Tools and materials
- 8 rolls wallpaper
- 24-inch level
- 2 gallons wallcovering adhesive
- lambswool roller
- wallpaper kit (which includes sponge, smoother, seam roller, trimmer tool, utility knife, and how-to guide) available at most paint stores, wallpaper showrooms, and home centers.

1 Establish a plumb line, which is a straight, vertical line. Use a level and pencil to mark the spot where you want to begin hanging paper. You can mark plumb lines around the room to ensure that all the strips hang straight. Then measure the height of the wall minus the baseboard and molding, and cut the paper into strips of that length, plus an extra 2 to 4 inches per strip; you'll need the extra length on the top and bottom for final trimming.

2 Place the first paper strip you'll apply to the wall pattern-side down on the work surface; allow the excess paper to hang over only one end of the table. Apply a thin layer of paste evenly over half of the strip with a roller. Follow the paper manufacturer's recommendations for the type of adhesive appropriate for your wallcovering. A heavy-duty clear wallcovering adhesive should be used along with a lambswool roller. Pour the paste into the glue tray and use the roller as you would a paint roller.

3 Book the pasted half of the strip (fold it over to the midpoint). This spreads the glue evenly and makes handling the strips easier. Then paste and book the second half. The pattern should now be facing up with the top and bottom edges meeting in the middle. Lightly press the glued sides together without creasing.

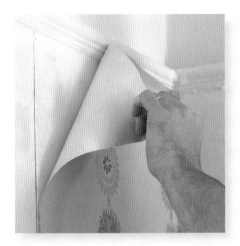

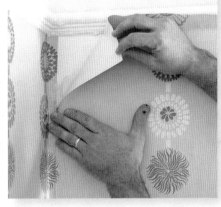

4 Align the vertical edge of the paper with the marked plumb line on the wall. Unbook the top half of the paper, leaving a 2-inch overlap at the top, and firmly press into place from top to midline. Smooth the paper against the wall with your hands. At the midline, unbook the rest of the strip and continue smoothing. Using a wide metal scraper as a straight edge, trim the top and bottom edges of the paper with a utility knife. Use a plastic smoother to flatten any wrinkles or air bubbles.

6 In some spots, you'll find that strips can't hang exactly parallel, especially in corners. In these areas, align the new strip by overlapping the edge of the old by about ½ inch (the extra ½ inch will wrap inside the edge of the corner to the other wall); be sure to match the pattern. Follow this procedure for all corners, and don't be tempted to use a single strip to wrap around the entire corner—it will eventually pull away.

5 Create a perfect seam. With hands flattened, place another strip of glued paper close to the affixed strip and gently slide it over until the two edges touch and the pattern is properly aligned. Use the smoother to thoroughly flatten the seam.

7 Trim excess paper around corners, moldings and the ceiling, drawing the utility knife along the metal scraper. Press and smooth paper to the wall. For tricky moldings, hang a strip that overlaps the frame by 2 to 3 inches. Cut a line from the tip of the corner molding to the edge of the paper. Fold down and mold paper to the corner, securing edges with a pushpin until dry.

GETTING STARTED

Measure the height and width of the space you wish to cover (excluding baseboards and molding) and round off to the next highest foot or half foot. Then ask the wallpaper retailer to compute the amount needed in your choice of paper. The dimensions and amount of wallpaper on a roll (also called a spool) vary according to makers. For patterned paper, you'll need a little extra to allow for the repeat (the dimensions of one complete segment of the repeating pattern) and to align the pattern properly. Before starting, remove furniture from the room or group everything in the center and cover with drop cloths. Set up a table or other clean work surface that's long and wide enough to hold long strips of paper.

PREPPING WALLS

Unless you prepare walls properly, every nick, hole and ding will show. So before you start papering, be sure to:

- Remove old, peeling wallpaper. Only paper over existing wallpaper if the material is adhered securely to the surface. If any edges are lifted or curled, glue down with wallpaper adhesive. Lightly sand seams so they won't show through the new paper.
- Remove curtain hardware, window treatments, switchplates and outlet covers.
- Repair any cracks and holes with spackling compound, and scrape off any loose paint.
- Sand down high-gloss-painted surfaces to create a dull finish.
- Wash off dirt and grime with household detergent; let dry before papering.

TRICKS FROM PROS

- You may notice slight color variations from roll to roll. To keep your wall color consistent, cut consecutive strips from a single roll and, before pasting, place them parallel to be sure the color matches.
- While working, keep your hands damp and the prep surface spotless.
- Paste, book, and hang one strip at a time. If the adhesive starts to dry before you have applied the strip, mist the glued side of the paper with water.
- After hanging each strip, step away from the wall and eye the paper to be sure it is straight. If it's crooked, gently pull from the corner for correct alignment.

PART 2

Kitchen Classics

Cooking, entertaining, living. These are the concepts most homeowners have in mind today when planning a kitchen remodel. They crave the amenities and conveniences that will enable them to utilize the space according to the way they live. They also want a style that pleases them and, most important, one that marries well with the overall style of their home and the furnishings they have assembled

Open design began to gain acceptance in the 1980s and still has resonance decades later. But there's a difference: instead of featuring flow-together kitchen-dining-family rooms, where no single space has dominion or its own specific style, today's kitchen designers focus on access. The kitchen may be separate, but it transitions easily into the dining room, the family room, the outdoor patio, even the pool deck. And more and more kitchens include family dining spaces—breakfast bars with comfortable stools or breakfast room extensions, some with built-in banquettes.

"The kitchen is part of a living environment," said renowned kitchen designer Ellen Cheever, addressing industry leaders in a panel discussion. "It's a place for cooking, of course, but there are also areas for gathering, perching, visiting. It's a multifunctional, multigenerational space." Cheever's take on kitchen design, as it relates to new as well as remodeled kitchens, was "Life goes on in the kitchen, rather than in the rooms next to the kitchen. More activities take place in the kitchen than eating or cooking." It may be an enclosed space, or one fully integrated into a home's living and entertaining areas, but the kitchen is no longer the preserve of a solitary cook. Thus it should be designed so that the whole family can get into the action. There should be handy storage and generous work space, to allow more than one cook to function comfortably. Note that the traditional work triangle has been pulled apart. "It's shaped more like an amoeba," said Cheever. And, although homeowners delight in cutting-edge appliances, they balk at design that makes a kitchen look like a lab.

Whatever its style, today's best kitchens hide all the high tech. And contemporary kitchen design is as much concerned with the flow of people in and out of the space as with getting food to the table. Most important, it is focused on individuality; making sure each space responds to the taste, style, and specific needs of the people who use it.

OPPOSITE: New furniture-style cabinets create a place for everything. Cabinet doors at the back of the room conceal a built-in pantry. Details like deep crown molding and bead board wainscoting reflect this home's traceable New England heritage.

TOP: Laminate counters, bottom-of-the-line cabinets and dated wallpaper were among the problems Suzann had to confront in her old kitchen. ABOVE: One oddity in the original space was a pair of freestanding electric ranges, placed at right angles to each other. LEFT: Moving the sink to a centrally located island and replacing one of the ranges with a built-in refrigerator helped create a more comfortable work area. A custom shelf lifted the microwave off the counter and out of the way.

History Reclaimed Suzann Murphy

believes that every old home should retain its historical character. Unfortunately, the previous owners of her family's century-old Watch Hill, Rhode Island, residence did not agree. They had stripped off all traces of its New England charm, replacing a time-worn wood floor with linoleum tile and exchanging the sturdy wood cabinets with unremarkable stock units. "It was so depressing," she remembers. "Shortly after we moved in, my husband and I painted the cabinets white, just to make the room feel more inviting."

But paint was only a temporary fix. The real problems with the kitchen were its awkward layout and lack of storage. "Nothing was in a logical place," says Suzann. "There were two freestanding ranges, but very little counter space. The refrigerator was a decent size, but it was a good 10 feet away from either cooking surface."

Enter Betsy House, owner of Kitchen & Bath Designs, a Stonington, Connecticut, design firm that specializes in classic kitchen remodels. It was House's job to not only restore the room's period charm, but also to make the space more appropriate for two homeowners who love to cook.

To improve the functionality of the room, House eliminated one of the two freestanding ranges, allowing her to move the refrigerator closer to the stove. Next, she reworked the plumbing so the sink could be taken off the wall and placed in a center island. The result is an easy-to-navigate work triangle with plenty of counter space. "Before, there wasn't even enough

The Wish List

- Replace builder-grade cabinets with furniture-style semi-custom units
- Move the sink from the wall to the freestanding island
- Convert a laundry room to a capacious pantry
- Install French doors to link the eating area to the backyard
- Add architectural details to restore the original character of the space

Storage Tip

Use the back of a kitchen island to its full storage potential by adding built-in shelves for cookbooks.

RIGHT: A custom hutch with built-in wine storage doubles as a bar when the Murphys entertain. The glass-front cabinets add visual interest; the wood counter adds warmth. BELOW: The original U-shaped kitchen lacked a central prep area, creating an awkward work space. Located between the sink and one of the ranges, a corner stairway contributed to the room's poor traffic pattern. BOTTOM: The remodeled kitchen has plenty of counter and storage space, both previously in short supply. Reworking the appliance layout helped the space function more efficiently.

room to stack dishes next to the sink," House said. All these adjustments made the room more chef friendly in every way but one: it reduced the amount of storage space. To remedy the situation, the designer converted a small laundry room into a double pantry, moving the washer and dryer into an adjacent bathroom.

With the storage issues addressed, House went to work restoring period personality to the space. She replaced the room's basic bottom-of-the-line cabinets with more furniturelike units. She also lowered the ceiling slightly to accommodate recessed lights and added beefy crown molding to create a finished look. Then she covered the backsplash with bead board and the wall behind the range with embossed metal tiles that resemble pressed tin. The Murphys were pleased with the historic look of their new kitchen, but it's the present-day efficiency of the center island that Suzann says she enjoys the most. "It's so nice to have everything so conveniently placed."

Space Saving

Jacob and Ayelet Kindler's suburban New Jersey kitchen had all the ingredients of a room desperate for a makeover. Measuring 250 square feet, it had minimal counter space, an awkward appliance layout, and dark-wood floor-to-ceiling cabinets. "Ayelet and I love to cook, but it was very difficult for both of us to use the room at the same time," Jacob says.

After living in their 1920s, Tudor-style house for a year, Jacob, a kitchen designer and owner of Home Solutions by D.S.K. Group, a New York City-based remodeling firm, came up with a plan for a more efficient and attractive kitchen. He did it by minimally altering the layout within the existing footprint. "Many people automatically assume that bigger is better," he said. "But after designing hundreds of kitchens—all 100 square feet or less—I'm inclined to disagree. Too much space can be just as hindering as too little; it encourages you to collect things that you don't need."

With that in mind, the room was gutted and rebuilt. Dark wood cabinets were replaced with custom white-painted units that offer a mix of open and closed storage. "One of our goals was to have the new kitchen tie in architecturally to the rest of the house," Jacob explained. "To do this, I replicated 1920s design elements, including cutouts at the base of the cabinets and an Art Deco–style range hood."

The combination of glass doors on the upper cabinets and open shelving helps to expand the space visually. A second window, added over the sink, lets in more sunlight. The new counters, walls, and backsplash areas are made of white 12-by-12-inch tiles. For a tighter, more efficient arrangement of elements, the range was moved to a position formerly occupied by the refrigerator, which was placed farther down the wall. The dishwasher and the refrigerator blend in beautifully with the cabinetry.

Finally, to add warmth to the space, Jacob replaced the old terra-cotta floor tiles with wood and added a wood dining table and storage cabinet. Making use of an otherwise dead space, he added several shelves at one end of the counter to hold Ayelet's collection of vintage rolling pins.

The new space has a small yet simple layout, still measuring 250 square feet, that successfully consolidates cooking and prep areas with plenty of room for guests and cooks to move around.

LEFT: The old kitchen featured dark wood cabinets and a rough tile floor. Its awkward layout made it hard for multiple cooks to share the space. RIGHT: Natural light pours in through the new windows and reflects off the white surfaces of the painted wood cabinets, tile wall treatment, and marble counters, giving the formerly cramped kitchen a bright, spacious appearance.

The Wish List

- Replace old cabinets with open shelves and custom cupboards with glass doors
- Remove the window over the sink and expand the opening by adding two new windows
- Integrate new appliances into the cabinetry to create a clean, unified look
- Rip out the old tile flooring and install a new wood floor
- Move washer and dryer to a room off the kitchen; replace with a bar sink and prep area

ABOVE: The new layout required surprisingly few structural changes. Jacob made the room more efficient by shifting appliances around and placing the island and its prep sink on a separate wall.

RIGHT: To make the small kitchen user friendly for more than one cook, Jacob redesigned the space that once contained a washer and dryer to create a small island-style prep center. BELOW: Glass doors and open shelving on the upper cabinets keep the space from feeling boxy. The wood floor, dining table, and china hutch bring warmth to the room.

Breathing Room

Almost as soon as Carla and Steven Nitz-Gamper moved into their suburban Atlanta split-level, back in 1993, they started planning a major kitchen remodel. Two years later, when hurricane Opal hit the Atlanta area, their dream of having a new kitchen had to be postponed—for nearly five years—while they repaired the extensive damage their house had suffered.

Instead of proceeding with their original plan, the couple did a quick fix during a two-month period, installing white-oak floors in the kitchen, dining area, and living room. The good thing about the wait, said Carla, a certified kitchen designer and owner, along with her husband, of Elementé Remodelers of Atlanta, was the time it gave them to plan their future kitchen. The project ended up winning the 2004 Chrysalis National Remodeling Award for best kitchen under $40,000.

For the new kitchen, Carla selected Shaker-style maple cabinets with a slightly aged finish, and topped base cabinets with warm-toned granite counters. The light maple and unadorned style of the cabinets have a contemporary feel. "Besides creating a new look," Carla commented, "we wanted to eliminate many of the old kitchen's shortcomings—like the peninsula with upper cabinets that blocked the view to the dining area."

Before

TOP: Slightly lowering the 46-inch cooktop put it at a more convenient height for the diminutive Carla. Increasing the wall space behind the range created an illusion that visually enlarges the kitchen. Below the cooktop, full-extension drawers were installed to hold pots and pans; the cabinet at right is designed to hold spices. ABOVE: Inadequate lighting and white cabinets and tiles combined to give the kitchen a stark feel. A temporary counter, shown here, was added for meal preparation and storage space during the remodeling.

The Wish List

- Increase the floor space by removing an intrusive dividing wall
- Add a 9-by-14-foot bumpout to the dining area; link to the patio with a sliding glass door
- Install white-oak floors and semi-custom natural maple cabinets
- Replace tile surfaces with granite counters and a limestone-tile backsplash
- Bring in new stainless steel appliances plus coordinating hardware

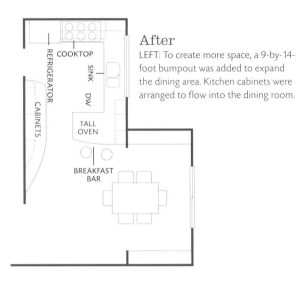

After

LEFT: To create more space, a 9-by-14-foot bumpout was added to expand the dining area. Kitchen cabinets were arranged to flow into the dining room.

Before

ABOVE: The wall between the living room and kitchen created a closed-in feeling. A tall wall oven, placed at the end of the peninsula interrupted traffic flow.

ABOVE: Before the major remodeling took place, the old peninsula was removed and the wall oven was shifted to the back. Makeshift storage was added above and below the oven. RIGHT: Frosted-glass cabinet doors above the hood break up the expanse of wood in the room. With counters on both sides of the sink and peninsula area, the kitchen has abundant space for multiple cooks.

For these homeowners, the most offensive element was a 6½-foot-tall dividing wall between the living room and kitchen that was topped with a brick planter filled with fake plants. "The whole area was cramped and inefficient," said Carla.

In addition to eliminating the dividing wall, the couple added a 9-by-14-foot bumpout to the eating space—the home's main dining area. Opening onto a patio, the space is now large enough to seat a dozen diners. The new addition also contains a built-in pantry, broom closet, and china cabinet, as well as plenty of storage space for crafts.

Cabinet interiors were customized to store dishes and cooking supplies at convenient heights for Carla's 5-foot-4-inch frame. To soften the room's angles, she incorporated a series of arcs and curves into the design; stainless steel appliances and hardware also add to the contemporary tone. "The combination of natural materials, good performance, and distinctive design made this a kitchen worth waiting for," Carla declared.

ABOVE: The new counter often doubles as a large buffet space for family meals or entertaining. Carla's husband, Steve, a talented woodworker, crafted the curved shelves at both ends of the upper cabinets. Locating the oven below the counter keeps sight lines open; the microwave is hidden in the upper cabinets. Lower cabinets have custom storage for big serving pieces and canned goods. Family photos are framed in red to pick up red flecks in the granite counters.

Made for a Cook

Designer Danelle Carnes, ASID, of Carnes Interiors in Albuquerque, New Mexico, waited ten years to redo her kitchen. She saved money and collected ideas so that when she was ready to make the leap, she would have her dream kitchen. Her one-story house, six miles from downtown, had been built in 1983. Unimproved since then, the kitchen needed more than just a face-lift. Danelle, who likes to cook and entertain, had wearied of a work triangle that had her hiking 23 feet across the kitchen to get from the refrigerator to the sink. She also wanted more usable work and storage room. With help from Tim Rizek, of Rizek Custom Homes & Remodeling in Albuquerque, Danelle created an all-new kitchen without the expense of taking down walls or moving the plumbing.

"Danelle was determined to work within the existing 11½-by-16-foot space," said Rizek. So space once devoted to a walk-in pantry was absorbed, as was the doorway leading to the water heater and heating system. To break up the expanse of her new custom red-birch cabinets, Danelle specified frosted-glass door fronts for some upper units. Unlike most wall cabinets, the doors open by swinging up, not out. Cabinets on the refrigerator wall were pulled 12 inches out from the wall itself. "That way, I could have 12-inch-deep appliance garages and still have a 24-inch-deep work surface," Danelle explained. For the floor, she chose cork, a natural product—sustainable and renewable—that is comfortable to walk and stand on. Recessed ceiling lights, under-cabinet lighting, and a pendant provide overhead and task lighting.

In the new layout, the appliances moved but the sink remained. In addition, a small vegetable sink was installed in the corner near the cooktop. "Now I can move from fridge to stove to sink in just a few steps," Danelle exulted. "This kitchen has everything I need."

ABOVE: The old kitchen had modest storage space, no style, and a card table that doubled as work space and breakfast bar. An unattractive bookcase with drawers held cookbooks and linens.

The Wish List

- Replace old cabinets, appliances, cabinets, countertops, and lighting
- Eliminate a walk-in pantry to make room for a new freestanding refrigerator
- Add a secondary sink for washing vegetables
- Install a fold-down desk in the dead space where a door leading to the heating system had been

LEFT: A major factor in the success of this kitchen remodel is the improved new access Danelle now has from the kitchen into the dining room.

ABOVE: Marble tops the counter on the peninsula that separates the kitchen and dining room. The other countertops are made from a composite that looks just like wood with a soft, matte finish.

Before

RIGHT: A walk-in pantry and door to the heating system wasted valuable wall space on one side of the kitchen. The old layout also left a large distance between the sink and the meal-prep area.

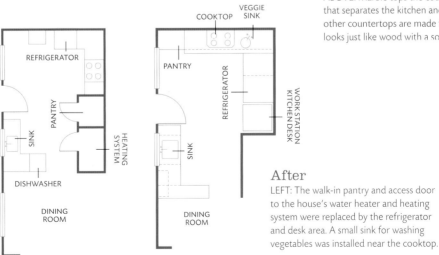

REFRIGERATOR

PANTRY

SINK

HEATING SYSTEM

DISHWASHER

DINING ROOM

COOKTOP   VEGGIE SINK

PANTRY

REFRIGERATOR

WORK STATION
KITCHEN DESK

SINK

DINING ROOM

After

LEFT: The walk-in pantry and access door to the house's water heater and heating system were replaced by the refrigerator and desk area. A small sink for washing vegetables was installed near the cooktop.

ABOVE: Danelle wanted the cooktop and built-in oven to be the kitchen's focal point. The backsplash consists of randomly placed 4-by-4-inch tiles in four colors. Counter-level cabinets behind the work space hide small appliances. RIGHT: Looking in from the dining room, the one item that stood out was a dated refrigerator that dominated the room. ABOVE, RIGHT: The vegetable sink beside the cooktop has a faucet with a pull-out nozzle. The sink itself is undermounted stainless steel with its own drain board. Danelle uses it as a spoon rest and as a place to put frozen foods in their final stage of thawing. FAR RIGHT: The frosted-glass wall cabinets have doors that rise upward. "They stay open in the up position," said the designer, "and are self-closing when given a gentle pull."

Before

PAINT AND DECORATE TILES

Tip
To protect tiles painted with latex or water-based paints, seal them with water-based floor varnish. Or you can paint the tiles with eggshell paint, which never needs varnishing.

Tools and materials
• sandpaper • paint brushes • tile primer • almond-white flat latex paint • waterbased floor varnish • curtain varnish • acrylic paint (to match fabric) • low-tack tape • transfer paper • pencil

1 Always check instructions for each product you use. After sanding the tiles, brush tile primer on both the tiles and the grout. Let it dry for at least 12 hours before applying paint.

2 Using an artist's brush, paint over the tiles and grout in almond-white flat latex paint. When dry, paint over some of the tiles in other colors. You may need two coats if you have chosen a dark color.

3 Once you have completed your design, allow paint to dry thoroughly. Then seal the latex paint with two coats of a strong water-based varnish.

4 Photocopy sections of the fabric you would like to use. This may be curtain fabric (as shown), tea towels or a tablecloth. Experiment with the patterns, enlarging or reducing each design element to the specific sizes you require.

5 Using low-tack tape, tape transfer paper over the surface where you want your design. Place the photocopy on top, tape in place, and trace over the outlines with a pencil. This will transfer it in a pale water-based ink, which you can paint over. Remove the paper and your design.

6 Using a fine artist's brush and acrylic paint, paint over the lines. If the design you want to transfer is not too intricate, you can paint it freehand. Don't worry about wobbly lines—they add to the charm. Allow the paint to dry, then finish off with two coats of varnish.

Elegance Uncluttered

Kitchen designer Pat Vuocolo, owner of Kitchens By Vuocolo in West Chester, Pennsylvania, had created her share of attractive and functional kitchens for clients. So, after spending a decade in her mid-1960s ranch-style home, she and her husband, Jerry, an avid cook, finally decided it was time to remodel their own small, dreary kitchen.

"Jerry and I have three grown children and seven grandchildren," Pat confided. "I wanted a kitchen that we could all be comfortable in, and one that would also serve as a showroom for my clients." Her 229-square-foot space was long, narrow, and difficult to work in. A cumbersome peninsula, out of proportion to the room, was first on the list to be removed. Then she added square footage by appropriating space from a nearby laundry area and removing an outside wall so that an extension could be built at one end of the kitchen.

Opening the room at this end also provided the opportunity for Pat to install casement windows, which she arranged so they would run the length of the room and wrap around the two corners. Extending the window arrangement not only improved the view but also ensured that the room would be filled with natural light.

Custom cherry cabinets replaced the standard maple cabinets installed forty years earlier. "The new cabinets were designed to provide plenty of

Before

TOP: Jerusalem gold tiles inset with pieces of granite create a focal point behind the hearth area. Built-in custom storage cabinets provide an organized space for cooking supplies. ABOVE: A lack of space and a dated look were two major problems with the previous kitchen. "We could barely move around the small prep area and the cramped breakfast space," Pat recalled.

ABOVE: The new sink has counter space on both sides, plus dishwasher drawers within easy reach. "I love that while I'm cleaning up I can enjoy the outdoor view," said Pat. "I also added a built-in soap dispenser to eliminate clutter on the counter." BELOW: With a built-in wine cooler, open display shelves, and roomy base cabinets, the new bar is a popular spot for guests. "We wanted an out-of-the-way spot where people could walk over to grab a drink."

ABOVE: Slide-out spice cabinets flank the hearth. This keeps everything organized and allows for a quick inside search. A small drawer under each spice rack holds pot holders. BELOW: A custom hutch with a built-in coffee and cappuccino maker solves a host of storage issues. "It's such a treat to serve a choice of coffees any time of day," said Pat. "I included storage cabinets in the hutch for dishes and drawers for utensils. Everything we need is right there."

The Wish List

- Open a wall at one end to expand the room
- Add as much as 10 square feet of cabinet space
- Install seven casement windows over the sink area
- Replace old appliances with all new pro-style models
- Create a new center island that includes an eating area

Before   After

FAR LEFT: The 229-square-foot kitchen was narrow and dominated by a large peninsula that was out of proportion to the rest of the room. LEFT: Relocating appliances and eliminating one wall improved the storage capacity and efficiency of the new kitchen.

Storage Tip

Make a list of the essential items that don't fit into your current kitchen and let those needs guide your remodel.

storage space as well as add richness to the room," Pat explained. Paying close attention to the use of space, she utilized the design of her cabinets in the most efficient way possible. "We never really had a proper place to store all of our pots and pans," she said. "I wanted to create cabinets that would include plenty of custom-designed drawers."

Built from the same cherry used for the cabinets, the new 3-by-10-foot center island is an important component of the new kitchen. "Having a small sink here makes preparing meals very easy," said Pat. On one end of the island there are display cabinets; on the other end, open shelves that provide space for cookbooks. The island is designed to accommodate four iron-backed chairs plus enough counter space for quick meals. Cream-colored granite with flecks of gold, brown, and black was used to top the island and adjacent counters. Continuing this natural color palette, Pat also selected cream-colored porcelain tile in different sizes for the floor. Because the kitchen is long and narrow—12½ feet at its widest point—she decided to stagger the floor tiles to create an optical illusion and eliminate a long railroad effect.

Improved lighting—including well-placed recessed fixtures, low-voltage under-cabinet lighting, and a three-light, Mediterranean-style pendant fixture over the island—illuminates the clutter-free space.

Pat's creative spark imbued the now 355-square-foot space with airiness and efficiency. The result is a kitchen functional enough for two people to work in simultaneously, and comfortable enough to be a family gathering spot.

BELOW: Built-in storage saves on counter space. A concealed TV on a swivel stand is located to the right of the hearth. "Jerry loves to watch his cooking shows while he works," said Pat.

HUTCH: BEFORE AND AFTER

Tools and materials

- screwdriver
- wax remover (if necessary)
- clean, lint-free cloths
- spackling compound
- putty knife
- sandpaper (220-grit)
- one 1-inch and three 2-inch foam brushes
- primer
- semi-gloss paint in two colors
- painter's masking tape
- round wooden door knobs

1 Remove the drawer, drawer pulls, and doorknobs from the hutch, leaving the doors open. If necessary, use wax remover and a cloth to remove wax buildup on the hutch and wipe down with a clean, damp cloth. Fill drawer pull holes with spackling compound. Lightly sand the hutch, and again wipe clean with a damp cloth.

2 Using a 2-inch brush, prime the hutch with a base coat to seal the wood. When thoroughly dry, lightly sand off any tiny air bubbles and wipe with a damp cloth.

3 Paint the inside of the hutch with two coats of the darker color, lightly sanding after the first coat is dry, then wiping clean with a damp cloth. Paint the outside of the hutch with two coats of the lighter color, lightly sanding after the first coat is dry and wiping clean with a damp cloth.

4 Use painter's masking tape to make two triangular shapes on the inset of the door panels so they remain the lighter color. Using the 1-inch brush, paint the unmasked portion of the door inset the darker color.

5 Prime the knobs, then paint with two coats of the lighter color paint, lightly sanding after the first coat. When dry, attach all of the knobs .

STOOL: BEFORE AND AFTER

Tools and materials

- wooden stool (if you don't have an old one, obtain an unfinished one)
- sandpaper (medium- and fine-grit)
- tack cloth
- primer (enamel, if your stool has lots of stains; otherwise, gesso works fine)
- 1- and 3-inch-wide synthetic brushes
- acrylic paint
- scissors
- a lightweight primed artist's canvas, 1½ inches wider than your stool
- artist's brush
- masking tape
- thick batting
- brass-plated upholstery nailheads

1 Sand stool evenly, first with medium-grit sandpaper, then with the fine. Wipe with a tack cloth between sandings.

2 Coat stool with primer, then let dry thoroughly.
3 Paint the stool in a color that works with what you will use for the canvas-covered seat pad. Let the paint dry.
4 Now, paint the primed artist's canvas with a light shade of paint. Let dry.
5 Starting at each short end of the canvas, apply strips of masking tape to form a consistent striped pattern—our stripes are 4 inches wide.
6 Between the tape strips, apply paint in a darker shade than your background. Remove masking tape, then let paint dry before adding the narrower stripes.
7 Using the artist's brush, paint thin contrasting stripes half an inch apart on the darker stripes. Let stripes dry.
8 Fold canvas edges over a piece of batting cut to fit stool top. Clip corners to miter, then place canvas over the stool, tacking it to the top with nailheads.

Functions Added

From every direction, the old kitchen in Susan Sherratt's Alameda, California, home conspired to confine her. A header dropped the ceiling height, a peninsula blocked off the breakfast nook to one side, and a peninsula with ceiling-hung cabinets blotted out a view of the family room. Having no windows added even more to the feeling of confinement.

Along with its significant cosmetic problems, the kitchen was essentially dysfunctional. What Susan really needed was an island work area instead of twin peninsulas. She was also frustrated by double wall ovens she considered to be a bit on the puny side. "I could barely get a turkey pan in either of them," she recalled. Susan's quest for bigger ovens drove her to remodel. Naturally, she and her husband, Richard, had other needs as well as an island: more storage, and, of course, aesthetic appeal.

Early in the process, Richard decided to add onto the space by having the breakfast nook wall pushed back, taking advantage of an overhang on the house. This eventually let kitchen designer Victoria Reginato, CKD, also of Alameda, expand the kitchen into the breakfast nook's old location. To open up the new space, Reginato removed the peninsula separating the kitchen and breakfast nook. She also evened up the ceiling heights, removing an unattractive dropped ceiling.

ABOVE AND BELOW: A load-bearing post with a header made room height seem low, as did the fluorescent light in the middle of the ceiling. A large refrigerator that protruded from the wall opposite the sink added to the crowded feeling.

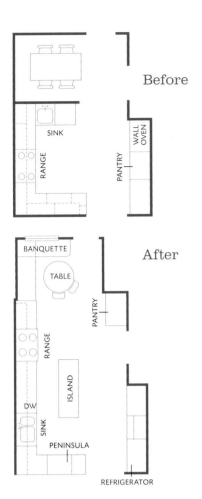

Before

After

BANQUETTE

TABLE

PANTRY

RANGE

ISLAND

DW

SINK

PENINSULA

REFRIGERATOR

SINK

RANGE

PANTRY

WALL OVEN

TOP: The old U-shaped kitchen had two peninsulas, each creating a clumsy barrier. The location of the sink on the peninsula near the breakfast nook, plus the placement of the range, created traffic flow problems—especially if more than one cook was at work. ABOVE: Changing to an L-shaped layout opened up the kitchen, as did adding floor space by pushing back the breakfast nook wall. OPPOSITE, TOP: Leveling the ceiling gave the new kitchen an expansive look. The L-shaped layout works nicely for both cooking and social functions.

TOP, CENTER: Susan turned the island into a baking center with a special built-in cabinet designed to lift her mixer to counter height. TOP, RIGHT: Above the sink, where a window might normally be placed, Susan hung a mural by local artists Janice Paredes and Sara Van Orsdel. "Another building lies just beyond the wall," said Reginato. "If we had put a window in there, we'd be looking at a brick wall." RIGHT: An expanse of polished granite surrounds an undermount sink equipped with a single-lever faucet. The dishwasher to the right of the sink is hidden behind a section of cabinet paneling.

"In the old kitchen, there was a load-bearing post with a header above it that made it feel like another room," Reginato pointed out. With help from a contractor, she moved the load from the header into the attic. "That got us a clean ceiling line from the kitchen into the family room, and that really made it feel like one big room."

Even with the expansion, the dimensions of the kitchen wouldn't allow a typical island. "The island is only one cabinet deep," Reginato explained. "That's not as deep as some might like, but we were able to create an island, which is what Susan wanted." And Susan made the island her baking center. "I had a cabinet built in to accommodate the mixer," she said. The mixer is on a shelf designed to lift up conveniently to counter height.

Confining no more, the space went from being a perennial eyesore to an expansive delight, a breakthrough that allows the Sherratts to get the most out of their kitchen.

ABOVE: Large double wall ovens and the refrigerator share a wall with a serving area, which features a built-in microwave. RIGHT: Extra storage is tucked into the breakfast nook banquette, which has drawers for stowing off-season items, extra dishes, and linens. The built-in seating also eliminates the need for extra chairs. Now there are only two rather than four—but there's still seating for six.

The Wish List

- Even out the ceiling heights by transferring the header load into the attic
- Extend the breakfast nook wall, adding 6 feet of space
- Install an island
- Replace the old wood floor with wide-plank hickory
- Put double ovens where a single oven had been
- Update the lighting, removing oversize fluorescent fixture

Stylish Update

For fourteen years, the owners of this 1892 home in Boston had lived with an outdated kitchen renovation done by previous owners. But when their oldest son went off to college, this commercial architect and his artist wife decided it was finally time to have the kitchen match the house's elegant style.

They began by seeking ideas from magazines, and came across a photo of a red kitchen, a color they felt would enliven their space. After the kitchen was gutted, cabinets were placed around the room. To improve work flow, appliances were moved to opposite walls, with the range, refrigerator, and main sink repositioned according to the plan's L shape. Also, red-oak flooring was reclaimed from a New England barn, and honed black granite counters were juxtaposed against a backsplash of gray slate tiles.

To obscure an unpleasant view without cutting off light, windows on the south-facing wall were replaced with a row of cabinets. Now, instead of staring at a garage, the owners are looking at beautiful cabinets. Above, fixed clerestory windows let in the sun; below-cabinet crank-out windows let in fresh air. For storage, lower cabinets all have deep pull-out drawers, and upper cabinets are 15 inches deep.

Unlike many kitchens, this one does not have a built-in island. "Because of the doorways, an island would interfere with the traffic flow," the architect-homeowner says. "We preferred the old-fashioned idea of a kitchen table, which fits the house's shingle-gambrel-roof Victorian style."

ABOVE: The custom cabinets and clever window-placement redesign are at the heart of the new kitchen. Built of ash, the cabinets were custom-stained a rich red. A band of natural-stained drawer fronts repeats the walls' soft yellow color.

Before

ABOVE: Poor layout and a lack of counter space made meal preparation an unpleasant chore.

The Wish List

- Replace old cabinets with custom units finished in a specially mixed red stain
- Install black granite counters, slate backsplash, new stainless steel appliances, and reclaimed oak floors
- Add generous-size storage areas, including a customized baking center
- Reposition windows to obscure an unsightly view
- Adjust appliance locations to create a better work flow

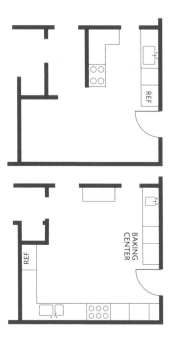

LEFT: In spite of its ample 16-by-17-foot size, the old kitchen had minimal storage space since all of the appliances were inconveniently placed in one small area. BELOW, LEFT: Cabinets line the walls, freeing up the middle of the room. With four doorways, bringing in a center island would have caused traffic-flow problems.

BOTTOM: A new baking center, overlooking the backyard, is placed against the wall that once housed the main sink and refrigerator. The counter was designed to be 37 inches high, one inch taller than normal to accommodate the tall homeowner who enjoys baking bread. The area has its own sink, a storage bin for flour, pull-out drawers for pans and bowls, and slots for baking sheets and racks.

LEFT: Assembling the family for some face time is not a chore with this two-bench table. It may bring to mind a diner booth, but the old setup was like a greasy-spoon counter, with family members facing front like so many lonely travelers. Now they can see each other as well as the fireplace, the water, and the mountains. BELOW: Kids can steer clear of the secondary work triangle thanks to a convection microwave, a full-size refrigerator, and an undercounter refrigerator that's been raised to make it a little more comfortable to use. People in the bar and dining room, both adjacent to this area, also make use of these appliances.

Fit for Family Living

Mealtime in this Mukilteo, Washington, home used to be a straightforward affair—everyone faced forward, that is. "There was only counter seating, with no other place to sit down," complained the homeowner. "When all four of us were at the counter, it felt like we were eating at a diner." Thus, a so-called family kitchen for four—the homeowners and their teenage son and daughter—was anything but family-friendly.

The original island was just big enough for the cooktop, with a skimpy prep area beside it. What's more, this cramped installation faced neither the family room, for cook-and-kids interaction, nor a drop-dead view of Puget Sound. As for the family room, the location of the windows and fireplace forced the television to the back wall so that the cook and family members actually faced in opposite directions.

With a banquette booth handling dining duties, the new kitchen encourages "interaction without interference," according to its designer, Sheila Tilander, of The Showplace Design & Remodeling in Redmond, Washington. By completely reconfiguring the space without enlarging it, she turned a white elephant into a welcoming kitchen, where mother and daughter can cook together with ease and the whole family can sit down together—face to face—for meals.

Tucked in a corner of the kitchen between the main sink and the refrigerator, a snack zone holds the microwave and an undercounter fridge, mainly for drinks, which family members can use without colliding with the cook. Tilander moved the cooktop to a peripheral counter, where its

LEFT: Two people—kids or guests—can belly up to the island's raised bar. The two-person seating limit here means that there is room for everyone to see and talk to one other, including whoever may be working at the sink or any other spot on this 4½-by-8-foot island. BELOW: Tilander's plan oriented the new kitchen to embrace a shamefully unexploited outdoor view and expand a too-tiny island, making it possible for a family of four to dine and live in spacious comfort.

Sound Ideas

• A microwave and an undercounter refrigerator installed out of the kitchen's main traffic pattern let family members help themselves to snacks without interfering with meal preparation. This snack zone is next to the dining room entrance, so the fridge doubles as a convenient beverage cooler for entertaining.

• Because a second oven would have gotten little use, a combination microwave and convection oven was chosen as a compromise.

• A shallow drawer under the cooktop holds skillets, freeing them from the indignity of being stored beneath various stockpots and saucepans.

• A motif of subtle graphic squares in the backsplash, range-hood accent tiles, banquette upholstery, and a pendant light above the banquette provides visual rhythm that helps bring unity to the large space.

ventilation hood doesn't create a visual obstacle. This and the main working counter are laminate, which the homeowner chose for its practicality. "So much pattern in granite makes it harder to see spills," she explained. Granite was reserved for the centerpiece 4½-by-8-foot island and the built-in banquette. The island, reoriented 90 degrees from the original (again, because of the view) and stretched in size, holds a prep sink with a second work zone, plus raised counter seating where kids or guests can perch.

To make a seamless transition from kitchen to family room, Tilander refaced the stone fireplace with porcelain tile and added a contemporary mantel of natural alder and walnut-stained cherry with stainless steel accents, the same materials used for the kitchen cabinets. A niche above the fireplace now holds a mirror but is wired for the flat-screen TV the family plans to purchase someday. Meanwhile, the current television occupies a custom cabinet behind the banquette, designed for easy conversion to storage as the audio-visual configuration evolves. That banquette is more than just another link to the family room. It's where the family gathers for meals, in a spot restaurant owners might sacrifice a limb for—in the glow of a fireplace, with a breathtaking view west to Puget Sound, Whidbey Island, and the towering Olympic Mountains.

ABOVE: Alder, a relatively little-used hardwood, provides the primary cabinet finish in this design, along with a little cherry. On the appliance front, the kitchen has a single convection oven and a warming drawer, a welcome addition. RIGHT: The banquette is placed to welcome the sun, especially in the late afternoon and evening. There, the family can hunker down for meals in front of a toasty fire and a majestic view. The niche above the fireplace is scaled to hold a flat-screen television.

Small Space Tip

To make a small kitchen look and feel larger, use the same material or the same colors on both cabinets and counters.

Charm Channeled

Growing up in an old farmhouse in the Indiana countryside, Stephanie Crick always knew she wanted to recreate the same down-home atmosphere in her own house. So when it came time to remodel the seven-year-old kitchen in her Indianapolis home, she jumped at the chance to incorporate the charming details she recalled from her childhood. "The kitchen is the anchor of our home," said Stephanie, who shares the space with husband, Terry, and their two children. Working with designer Michael Teipen, of Kitchens by Teipen in Greenwood, Indiana, Stephanie developed a checklist that included finding space for the family of four to share informal meals together.

Teipen obliged by carving out a half-moon-shaped chunk from the back side of the bi-level island—large enough to create a cozy banquette that wraps neatly around an antique pine table. "It was almost like fitting together two interlocking puzzle pieces," he said, describing the island's unique design. "We liked it so much, we repeated the circular motif in valances over the sink and range area. The island is also equipped with a prep sink, plus warming and refrigerated drawers, where Stephanie stocks exotic ingredients like her stash of imported chocolate. "The kids know never to go into Mommy's refrigerator, however," she said. "It's definitely off-limits."

Since the couple entertain frequently, Teipen worked with them to design a separate wine bar flanked by elaborate finial-topped towers. Crafted of alder wood, the piece has "all the detailing of a fine antique," the designer explained. To keep the space from becoming too formal, the owners chose custom maple cabinets with a hand-rubbed antique ivory finish and carved, furniture-style legs, which impart a feeling of age. To complement the room's whitewashed tones, they selected an ivory-and-gray open-pattern granite for counters and removed a bowling-alley-yellow finish from the oak floor, restoring it to its original tone.

"I couldn't be happier," said Stephanie, extolling the new space. "I wanted it to be user-friendly, and it is. It's user-welcome as well!"

BELOW: Six burners, a griddle, and two ovens make this pro-style range capable of cooking for quite a crowd. Countertop segments on either side of the appliance provide storage and offer opportunities for guests to do prep work without interfering with whoever is at the range or the island sink.

ABOVE: The griddle on this range can fill in as counters space when not serving its primary function. Above it, the swing-out pot-filler faucet is positioned to save gallons of time and effort. RIGHT: The half-moon-shaped banquette is carved out of the back of a massive bi-level island. The table is antique pine. Arcs over the range and the sink pick up on the half-moon theme.

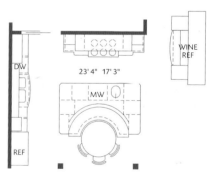

ABOVE: Its role as kitchen table makes the island seem massive, but the kitchen still has room for a hearth, and a wine bar, plus a separate prep and clean-up counter with its own sink. LEFT: The island includes a microwave oven built in at a kid-friendly height. It also has a warming drawer (below the microwave) as well as a prep sink.

Dining by the Numbers

Although no hard-and-fast rules exist, designer Michael Teipen offered the following guidelines to consider when planning a dine-in space:

- Allow 24 inches at the table per adult per setting. Two children can often squeeze into one adult spot.
- Plan on a total of 10 linear feet minimum to accommodate five people at an island comfortably.
- Provide at least 15 inches of depth for islands and breakfast bars. "Actually, 18 inches is better because you won't bump your knees," Teipen added. When entertaining, those extra inches allow more room to spread out a buffet, too.

ABOVE: Spices reside in an easily accessed pull-out cabinet to the right of the range. TOP, RIGHT: As a visual counterpoint, the wine bar cabinets are made of alder, although this area has antique-style details, too. RIGHT: Custom maple cabinets in a hand-rubbed ivory finish with open, carved furniture-style legs enhance the old-fashioned farm look. All three faucets in the room—at this sink, the island sink, and the pot filler at the range—have an aged-look antiqued finish.

KITCHEN CHAIR: BEFORE AND AFTER

Tools and materials
- sandpaper (220-grit)
- steel wool
- clean cloth or tack cloth
- two 1-inch and two 2-inch foam brushes
- semi-gloss paint in four shades of a single color
- painter's or low-tack masking tape
- primer
- artist's brush

1 Sand the chair and use steel wool to smooth the irregular surfaces. Wipe down with a damp cloth or tack cloth.
2 Prime the chair with a base coat to seal any bare spots. Let dry.
3 Using the 2-inch foam brush, paint

Before

the entire chair with the next to the lightest paint color.
4 With painter's tape, mask the argyle pattern on the back rest, placing tape at the edge of the pattern. Use the 1-inch foam brush and the next to the darkest shade of paint for the two outer diamond shapes. With the artist's brush, use the same paint to highlight selected details of the chair. Use the lightest color to paint the remaining diamond pattern. When the pattern is dry, remove the tape and use the artist's brush to paint zigzag stitching lines in the lightest and darkest shades.

FARM TABLE: BEFORE AND AFTER

Tools and materials
- sandpaper (220-grit)
- clean, lint-free cloth
- six 2-inch foam paintbrushes
- primer
- semi-gloss paint in five complementary shades
- painter's or low-tack masking tape, 1 inch wide
- pencil
- yardstick
- polyurethane, semi-gloss finish

1 Clean and sand the table. Wipe it with a clean damp cloth, then prime it. When dry, lightly sand the table and wipe off any sand dust with the damp cloth.
2 Choose five colors of paint, with color A the lightest and color E the darkest. Use color A for the background of the tabletop. Use color D, the next to darkest color, for the underside of the table, legs, crosspiece, and for three squares on the tabletop. Use colors B, C, and E for three squares each on the top.

3 Paint the tabletop with two coats of color A, lightly sanding after the first coat and wiping clean. Paint the underside of the table, the table legs and the crosspiece with two coats of color D, lightly sanding after the first coat and making sure to wipe clean with a damp cloth.
4 Place masking tape around the outside edge of the tabletop to create a 1-inch border. Then use masking tape to divide the tabletop into 12 equal squares. Use colors B, C, D, and E to paint three squares each, applying two coats of paint to each square. (Colors in the picture, going from far end to near end and from left to right are as follows: row one colors B, E, D, and C; row two colors D, C, B, and E; row three colors E, B, C, and D.) Carefully remove the masking tape when painting is complete, and touch up if necessary.
5 When the tabletop is dry, brush on two coats of polyurethane, lightly sanding after the first coat dries.

Before

Opened Up

Located in the small waterfront community of New Buffalo, Michigan, Steve and Janet Dahl's cottage-style condo is an ideal place to chill out. Steve, a popular Chicago radio personality, and Janet, a homemaker, have three grown sons and frequently host family and friends at their weekend home.

Since their dark, closed-off 185-square-foot kitchen made party-giving a chore, the couple asked Kathy Hoffman, of Susan Fredman & Associates in Union Pier, Michigan, to design a more functional, welcoming kitchen within the existing footprint. Removing two walls and tweaking the floor plan opened up new possibilities and added more light. Said Hoffman, "We wanted to create a sunny space that would favor family gatherings and also hew to a color palette that would reflect the condo's natural surroundings."

Before

LEFT: Dark wood and dated wallpaper were only two of the Dahls' objections to their old kitchen. ABOVE: Part of a multi-unit condominium, the kitchen had to be remodeled within its existing footprint. Specifying pale painted cabinets and painting the walls a light khaki helped brighten the space.

Check Out the Details

- ISLAND The two-level center island has storage drawers, a double sink, a dishwasher, and seating.
- CABINETS White-painted maple cabinets with bead board detailing and a coffee glaze replace dark wood cabinets that made the old kitchen seem dreary.
- FLOORING Country-grade maple flooring is in line with the kitchen's specified light look.
- COUNTERTOPS Earth-tone granite countertops are inspired by the pebbles and sand right outside.
- BACKSPLASH Part of the kitchen's subway-tile backsplash was laid horizontally, while other sections were laid in a vertical pattern for visual interest.
- BUILT-IN BANQUETTE The new floor plan made room for a corner banquette. Its seats are hinged for access to storage underneath.

Lifted With Light

Surrounded by woods, Steve and Megan Dragich's two-level New Buffalo, Michigan, vacation getaway has a traditional look. But after owning this home for a couple of years, the couple—with one child in high school and another in college—decided it was time to give their standard-grade 200-square-foot kitchen a makeover.

Keeping the exterior walls in place but replacing the cabinetry were the key changes that brightened the space. "They wanted to upgrade and update, to make the kitchen more of a focal point for entertaining," said their designer, Karen Garlanger Straub, of Susan Fredman & Associates. They also created a visual link to the living room by repeating its maple flooring, which reinforced the flow between the two spaces.

Before

LEFT: The existing kitchen was bland and gloomy, with laminate counters, basic cabinets, and a dark tile floor. BELOW: White-painted window frames around the sink and glazed maple cabinets brighten the room. A liplike extension allows the granite countertop to double as a breakfast bar.

Check Out the Details

- **CABINETS** Custom natural maple cabinets and made-to-order bronze hardware that patinas with age add richness to the kitchen. A new pantry beside the panel-front refrigerator pulls out for storage. Glass-front cabinets by the window lighten the look of the room.
- **COUNTERTOPS** The granite countertops are a major upgrade from the old white plastic laminate. These are tan with touches of white, plus burgundy—a color used liberally in the adjacent living room.
- **ISLAND** With a drop-in cooktop, seating for two, under-counter storage, and a built-in wine rack, the island is a workhorse. Decorative legs give it a furniture look.
- **SINK** The white farmhouse sink is an informal touch. A tea-colored mosaic tile backsplash draws the eye and also adds a bit of sparkle.

ABOVE: The old island had a smooth cooktop on one side that could be dangerous with kids around. LEFT: The new kitchen has a separate range plus a 15-foot-long island with a double sink, counter space for four, and a raised work zone..

Making Room

While many kitchen remodels are intent on improving the look of a room, John Bryant Snell and his wife, Jamie Moldafsky, of St. Joseph, Michigan, had a different concern: better function.

"As a professional chef, John really wanted to separate his meal-prep, cooking, and baking areas," said Barbara Ince, a designer based in the Chicago office of Susan Fredman & Associates. Because of Jamie's job with a major appliance manufacturer, she and John could take advantage of the opportunity to test—and seriously consider—a number of quality appliances. To accommodate all the upgrades, the kitchen was gutted, and extra space was created by absorbing an existing breakfast room, no longer needed.

The couple, parents of two young children, now had room enough for everything they had dreamed of in a high-performance gourmet kitchen, plus a wall of windows placed to flood the room with natural light.

Check Out the Details

- APPLIANCES Double ovens, a combination microwave and convection oven, two dishwashers, and two large pro-style built-in refrigerators are only some of the gourmet features. "There's also a six-burner range alongside a six-burner cooktop with a custom exhaust hood, and stainless steel cabinet below," according to designer Ince.

- CABINETS A natural cherry finish with sleek satin nickel pulls give the kitchen the industrial flavor John and Jamie wanted. Open shelves above the coffee center-breakfast area provide easy access to cups and bowls. The pantry door features a chalkboard paint insert that allows John to post menus when planning dinner parties.

- LIGHTING Under-cabinet lights, recessed cans, and a hanging fixture over the island illuminate work spaces. New windows improve views and bring in plenty of natural light.

Light Fantastic

Whenever a lightbulb goes on over a cartoon head, it means someone has an idea. In the real world, you need to have all your ideas about lighting your new kitchen before the lights go on.

"Lighting is one of the most misunderstood aspects of kitchens today," said Bruno Pasqualucci, of Mohawk Kitchens in Stamford, Connecticut. Too many homeowners settle for the typical solution: a fluorescent ceiling fixture that casts a harsh glare. Creating layers of light with three types of lighting—general, task and accent—can make a kitchen more functional and attractive.

Ambient, or general lighting, such as recessed ceiling canisters, illuminates the whole kitchen. Task lighting—hanging pendants or strips placed under cabinets—focuses on work surfaces and should be considered a staple in a lighting plan. Accent lighting, often mounted in a soffit above the cabinets, can create a soft glow that washes the wall and ceiling.

ABOVE, LEFT: Individual pendant fixtures work well in tall spaces such as kitchens with cathedral ceilings. They enhance design and bring light close to surface areas. ABOVE, RIGHT: Light can behave unpredictably in kitchens with multiple reflective surfaces—polished stone counters for example. A lighting professional can advise on the optimal lamps and luminaires to use in these situations. BELOW: Three windows installed at the end of the room brighten up the breakfast area. The pendant light fixtures help define specific areas of use.

A SPATE OF CHOICES

Lighting technology evolves constantly, and options exist to fit every budget and design. Fluorescent tubes, popular for their low cost and low heat, now come in versions that cast a warmer color, comparable to that of incandescent bulbs. Some designers are using xenon lamps instead of halogen bulbs in recessed cans. Xenon is a little more expensive, but it doesn't produce as much heat as halogen, and the bulbs are similarly long lasting.

Lighting technology once reserved for commercial projects is now dazzling homes as well. Neon, or cold cathode, typically associated with colorful advertising, is an emerging choice for accent lighting in coves and soffits. Although the fixtures have an extended lifetime, they remain pricey for use in small areas.

Fiber-optic lighting is also gaining acceptance. Mounted inside cabinets or under shelves, it's a spectacular way to bring color—or multiple colors—to the kitchen. Light travels through a translucent or perforated hose, which typically runs along a soffit. Mick de Giulio, of de Giulio Kitchen Design in Chicago, recalled installing a fiber-optic color wheel in a ceiling cove. Controlled by a timer, the light continually glowed from red to green to blue to yellow.

ABOVE: Sometimes lighting functions can be combined, as in this cooking alcove, where a pair of small pendants illuminate a work surface and add decorative flair to the kitchen. BELOW: A variety of lighting is used throughout, top-hat canisters create general light, undercabinet lighting illuminates countertop tasks and pendants accent the island.

SUBTLE ACCENTS

It's the subtlest gestures that make a kitchen sparkle. Mike Noon, of Palindrome Lighting Design in Gambrills, Maryland, has favored using low-voltage lighting to spotlight fine fixtures such as a crystal chandelier, a luxurious touch for a high-end kitchen. "When you run the lights of the chandelier at the dim level and shine the room light on the chandelier, you get the full effect of the sparkling glass with no glare," he declared. De Giulio has been using the newest recessed-can models; with no baffle or trim, the ceiling can be dry-walled right up to the opening for a clean look.

A good lighting plan is easy on the eye, and the kitchen is the one place in the home where it's critical to get it right. "The best way to gather ideas is to visit lighting showrooms, look at fixtures, and see the effects," de Giulio advised. "Then you can make judgments based on exactly what you like."

FROM TOP TO BOTTOM: Particularly in a space that is short on natural light, dimmer systems can help create a variety of different lighting situations within a room: ambient, task, and accent. When choosing light fixtures for your kitchen, make sure your selection relates to other details and materials in the room, such as cabinet style and hardware. Retrofitting under-cabinet lights is effective in boosting a kitchen's efficiency. Plug-in models can get you out of the dark, fast; hard-wired fixtures demand a more complex installation, but yield a cleaner look and, often, increased function.

Know Your Bulbs

Different types of bulbs generate different colors and intensities of light, and some fixtures are designed to take specific types of bulbs. Always use the same color bulb throughout a room to ensure a consistent look.

INCANDESCENT Inexpensive general-service bulbs that produce a yellowish-white light; available in clear or frosted glass, and in a variety of wattages and shapes.

TUNGSTEN-HALOGEN Has a longer life and provides more light per watt than incandescent bulbs; emits a bright white light from bulbs available in various voltages.

Lighting Your Way Brilliantly

Make sure your kitchen has the right mix of accent, task, and ambient lighting so you can avoid these pitfalls:

BLACK HOLE An opening in a room that appears to be empty, especially at night, because there is insufficient illumination to light up the whole space.

GLARE BOMB A blast of bright light that inadvertently becomes the focus of attention, typically a single light source placed in the middle of a room.

MUSEUM EFFECT The result of too much accent light directed to the sides of a room. Just as with a glare bomb, the focus of the light is misplaced and can cause eye fatigue.

SWISS-CHEESE EFFECT Too many apparent holes in the ceiling from an overabundance of recessed fixtures.

FLUORESCENT Lasts up to twenty times longer than incandescent bulbs and gives off a comparable amount of light while using one fifth to one third the electricity; available in a broad spectrum of colors, shapes, and sizes.

XENON A long-life, low-wattage incandescent source, operated at low voltage and typically used as under-cabinet task lighting. Linked to appropriate controls, xenon sources are dimmable, thus offering a range of light levels.

NEON/COLD CATHODE A type of fluorescent lighting generally custom-made for continuous lighting of ceiling coves. Neon and cold cathode sources are dimmable with appropriate controls.

FIBER OPTICS A type of remote-source lighting wherein the light source is physically separated from light output, and light travels down a fiber bundle to be distributed into the room.

The homeowner wanted a spacious contemporary kitchen with lots of cabinets and counter space. He decided to run the cabinets up to the ceiling to make the space seem larger.

Before

TOP: The large pass-through from kitchen to dining room expands the space visually and makes it easier to interact with guests. ABOVE: George disliked the floral wallpaper, builder-grade cabinets, and strictly basic appliances that came with the kitchen. The room also had inadequate counter space, a challenge when cooking and entertaining.

Smart Alterations
When George Marrone bought his three-story, contemporary-style home in the Philadelphia suburb of Aston, Pennsylvania, he knew he needed to make some changes to the existing 120-square-foot kitchen. "The room just didn't suit my style," said George, who shares his home with partner Michael Nocera. "It had lots of flat surfaces, but very little work space, no island, and no seating area. The room also had a large pantry that took up an entire wall." Hoping to create a more practical layout, one conducive to cooking as well as entertaining guests, George fashioned his own detailed plan for upgrading the space.

Doing most of the work himself, he gutted the entire kitchen, replacing the nondescript cabinets with semi-custom maple units in a natural finish, a move that totally transformed the look of the space. "I installed a thin strip of crown molding on top, subtle enough to add interest to the surface yet maintain a contemporary feel," he said. To add prep space and open storage, George installed a freestanding island sized perfectly to the scale of the room. He also replaced the pantry with a breakfast area.

For surface interest, he used a mix of materials. Black granite tile was picked for flooring to contrast with the blond cabinets. Cabinet hardware mimics the finish on the stainless steel dishwasher and wall oven handles. For the backsplash, George opted for a brushed stainless alloy mosaic tile, providing a strong visual break between the black granite counters and wood cabinets. "I wanted to avoid bringing color into the room," he confided. "I made up for the lack of it by adding lots of texture."

Wanting a seamless look, George chose a cooktop and wall oven instead of a bulky range, and made sure the refrigerator was flush with the cabinets. "As it's a small space, I decided to keep things simple," he said. Other touches include natural bamboo blinds, a durable sisal-like rug, and undercabinet lighting to brighten task areas. These accessories help pull the space together and create an chic, urban feeling. "My goal," George explained, "was to create a contemporary kitchen that would not only work for me but also be a warm and welcoming place for friends and family."

The Wish List

- Gut the old kitchen
- Upgrade the electrical and plumbing systems
- Replace builder-grade cabinets with more useful semi-custom maple cabinets
- Install black granite counters and black granite floor tiles
- Add new professional-style stainless steel appliances
- Paint the walls a warm gold
- Include an island with a wood top and open storage below

BEFORE The kitchen's original layout lacked counter space and sitting room. One wall was dominated by a pantry that was just too large for the room.

AFTER Adding an island and a breakfast area, moving the dishwasher closer to the sink, and replacing the single sink with a double basin all helped create a more user-friendly kitchen.

Storage Practicalities

1 Knives stored on a magnetic board keep them easily accessible but out of the way.

2 A pull-out trash can concealed in a cabinet to the right of the oven frees up floor space and keeps unwanted odors under control.

3 A handy pull-out pantry to the left of the oven provides much-needed storage for a variety of packaged favorites.

ABOVE: Cabinets in the original kitchen floated awkwardly on the range wall, providing little storage. Counter space was also reduced both by the placement and the size of the range. LEFT: The pantry cupboard at the edge of the range wall and large drawers on either side of the range are custom outfitted for optimum storage. The subtle arch in the tile backsplash behind the range echoes the arch in cabinetry flanking the exhaust hood.

Extracting Potential

This Atlanta kitchen had everything the homeowners needed, an adequate layout, abundant light and ample space. The problem was its decidedly lackluster appearance—especially the original builder-grade white stock cabinetry and worn solid-surface counters.

Working with designer Amanda Johnson, of Atlanta's Small Carpenters at Large, the owners agreed on a design that would improve the kitchen without changing its layout. To keep the cost down, they ultimately decided to preserve the existing wood flooring and minimize any changes to the ceiling or lighting plan.

"This project gave the homeowners an up-to-date yet classic kitchen, one that preserved the positive aspects of the space," says Johnson. The designer started by replacing the drab cabinetry with custom maple cabinets that extended to the ceiling. The new cabinets featured inlaid door panels, rope and crown molding, end panels and decorative feet that created the appearance of fine furniture.

A new island with a single-level countertop and custom detailing replaced an existing split-level island that wasted valuable counter space. Installing a smartly integrated pantry cupboard helped eliminate the bulky projection of a former pantry closet. What's more, placing the pantry

The Wish List

- Remove old stock cabinets and replace them with custom maple units
- Extend cabinetry up to the ceiling to maximize storage
- Replace an awkward pantry closet with an integrated pantry cupboard
- Create a column-topped cabinet to visually divide the kitchen from the family room
- Bring in granite and wood to replace old countertops made of solid surfacing

Before

ABOVE: The original white cabinetry wasted storage space by stopping short of the ceiling. The oversize refrigerator held a lot but became a catch-all for paper clutter. OPPOSITE: Glass-front details in the upper cabinets prevent a top-heavy appearance. Designer Johnson suggested adding panel detailing to the back of the island to ensure an attractive view from the breakfast area. RIGHT: The column-topped cabinet provides storage on the kitchen side and a place to arrange furniture on the family-room side. The wood countertop, rope detailing, and feet add to the look of fine furniture.

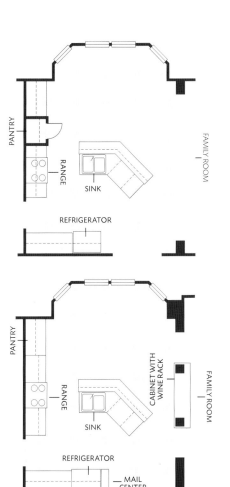

cupboard at the end of the range-wall run of cabinets made room for more countertop space. Finally, an elegant new sideboard-like cabinet separated the family room from the kitchen.

Other small touches added up to making a big difference. A chocolate-colored glaze on the cabinets, creamy off-white tiles, and handsome granite-and-wood countertops all lend warmth to the space. A well-placed spotlight highlights art and flower displays on top of the sideboard cabinet. And clever storage ideas, like a two-tiered pull-out utensil cupboard, wine storage grid, and phone and office cubbyholes make this kitchen as efficient as it is attractive. "The old kitchen was a nondescript space," Johnson remembered, "but now it's a highly functional focal point of the home."

Before

ABOVE, LEFT: The kitchen was completely open to the family room, with no visual break, exposing the entire room to a not-very-appealing view of one side of the refrigerator.

After

LEFT: A low cabinet placed between the kitchen and family room supplies bonus storage, plus additional counter space. The cabinet also acts as a subtle but attractive room divider.

Tip

Sample a color before you commit to it, especially for such big-ticket items as cabinets. Tape pieces of similarly colored construction paper to old cabinets and live with the look for a while.

PART 3

Bathroom Beauties

They used to be secrets. People once spoke of bathrooms in whispers. They were private spaces, and when they were pictured—in ads, magazine stories, or real estate listings—no toilet was ever shown. Today, bathrooms are talked about openly and honestly. In essence, they have come out of the closet. We have grown up, it seems. And when we plan a new or remodeled bathroom, we can state exactly how much storage space we need and how high our sinks, countertops, and toilets should be.

Like kitchens, bathrooms have traditional practical needs: plumbing, lighting, heating, and wiring, Those are the basics. Today, there are many more considerations, for bathrooms have gone beyond the realm of pure functionality and entered the world of style. Color is a top consideration, since homeowners consider color choices as important as layout, cabinet style as significant as elbow room. It was not long ago that the average home had one family bathroom plus maybe one lav. Today's homes have guest baths, children's baths, powder rooms, and often lavish baths as part of separate master suites. The bath as serene retreat is now high on the list of much-wanted particulars. A basic bath such as our parents and grandparents knew exists today mainly in homes in need of renovation.

We don't have just bathtubs; we have spas—tubs that, aided by water or air jets, create soothing bubbles; baths with built-in TV's or music systems; baths that boast of hydrotherapy, chromatherapy, or aroma therapy. Showers no longer feature just one spray; some have body sprays, foot baths, and, of course, shower heads as huge as sunflowers. Toilets have lids that rise and fall automatically, and in an age fraught with environmental concerns, some flush fast and powerfully, using barely more than a gallon of water each time.

Remodeling a bath is not like redecorating a living room. The elements are mostly fixed. Making changes is never as simple as moving a sofa. Some bath remodels are as minimal as replacing old faucets and applying new paint. Others are more dramatic: opening up walls or changing windows, tile, and every fitting and fixture. You needn't do a lot to make a big difference. Fresh towels could brighten your outlook; a new vanity might hold all your gear. Whatever you do, know that fashion shouldn't govern your choices, your own needs and style are all that really count.

OPPOSITE: Pristine and elegant, this 6-foot-wide shower stall, encased in cool glass tile, has a large overhead spray and an adjustable hand shower. Low-voltage halogen spotlights brighten the space.

Before

ABOVE: Over the years, the bathroom's structure had deteriorated so badly from water damage that the floor joists and window frame were completely rotted and had to be replaced. The old claw-foot tub had rust around the drain plus years of grime that had stained the worn enamel finish. It was replaced with a built-in tub. BELOW: Due to limited wall space, a towel bar was placed inside the tub area. The window shade is water-resistant vinyl.

Vintage Revival

This jewel box of a bath is a modest part of a long-awaited whole-house renovation. After thirteen years in their 1920s bungalow in Denver's Washington Park neighborhood, the homeowners were more than ready to make changes. They had interviewed local architect Doug Walter when they first moved in. "My husband and I knew right away that he had the vision we were looking for," said the owner, Joan Deming, but the cost estimate was too high at the time. Charmed by Walter's history of sensitive renovations, however, the Demings saved up so that, eventually, they could afford to hire him and do the job right.

Today, there are no remnants of the original bath, not even the claw-foot tub. "Actually, the homeowners were happy to make the switch since the tub's finish was shot," Walter recalled. The octagonal porcelain tiles look convincingly old but are actually brand new. Working within a historic context, Walter avoided specifying expensive materials—such as granite or marble—not typical of vintage bungalow style. Joan loved the idea of a black-and-white theme. "It was a nostalgic choice—I grew up in a home with black-and-white linoleum tiles," she recalled.

Remodeling, but also bringing the bathroom back to refined simplicity, proved challenging. Aside from being confined to an unalterable footprint, a diminutive 5½-by-5½-foot space, Walter discovered rotted floor joists and a rotted wood window, forcing him to strip the room down to its studs. He made the needed repairs and, with ceiling and walls open, seized the opportunity to add modern amenities, like ground-fault plugs, recessed lighting, and a ventilation fan.

An architect trained in home restoration and preservation, Walter produced a plan focused on creating an ambiguity in every room, particularly the bathroom. "We wanted visitors to ask: Is it new? Is it old?" Walter insisted "We got what we wished for," Joan said "Friends always want to know if we uncovered the original floor in the bath. We didn't."

The Wish List

- Pull everything out; strip the room down to its studs, beams, and floor joists
- Tile the walls surrounding the tub all the way to the ceiling as a setting for an in-bath shower
- Replace the worn, stained claw-foot tub with a new drop-in model
- Change forced-air heating to a more effective and energy-efficient hot-water baseboard system
- Replace the rotted wood-frame window with vinyl
- Add recessed lighting above the toilet and tub

Laced with Color

Their children now grown, it was time for Steve George and Sharon Capuano-George to create a new look for their empty nest, a small 1940s bungalow in St. Paul, Minnesota.

Steve, general manager of Authentic Construction in St. Paul, began by turning a small, inefficient upstairs bathroom into a master bath suite with a capacious closet and dressing room. "Now we can enter the bathroom through a walk-in closet or enter through a hallway door," he explained.

The remodeled bathroom occupies the same area as the old one, but Steve reconfigured the space by rotating the toilet and installing a shower where there had once been a doorway. The shower and tub area are clad in a blue-green porcelain tile of varying dimensions, a look that complements the rich red walls. Custom built-in maple cabinets that look like furniture were added to provide storage as well as create an architectural divider between the bathroom and dressing room.

"To ensure that the floor of the wet area was even with the wood floor in the vanity and dressing areas," Steve explained, "a cement base was put in, then tile was installed on the same plane as the hardwood floor." During the process, an in-floor heating system was installed in the areas surrounding the shower and bath.

Top Tip

"Don't hesitate to consider your age," Steve advised. "If you have trouble bending over or rising from a sitting position, install a vanity that is 36 inches high instead of 32 inches, and put in a high boy toilet that is taller than most standard models."

BELOW: Repositioning the toilet made room for a built-in combination bookcase and storage unit. Made of maple, it does double duty as a wall divider between the bath and dressing room.

Before

The Wish List

- Transform a small bathroom into a combination master bath, walk-in closet, and dressing room
- Install a 1-inch concrete base so the bathroom's new floor tiles would be even with adjacent wood floors
- Customize a floor-to-ceiling unit that includes a bookcase and a series of small storage drawers
- Remove fixtures and wall tiles and replace them with new tiles, tub, toilet, shower, and a 36-inch-tall vanity
- Install shelves above the tub area as a decorating touch and also to add storage space

Before   After

ABOVE, LEFT: The old bath had scant space between the toilet and tub. And the sink was barely big enough for one person to use. Unattractive metal wall tiles had been painted over. ABOVE: Solid surfacing was used for both the countertop and shelving. Fanciful figures serve as cabinet pulls and towel hooks. The 3-by-5-foot shower features a swinging door fitted with 3/8-inch tempered glass. FAR LEFT: The old bath and master bedroom were formerly not connected. LEFT: In the new plan, a 45-square-foot bath became a 100-square-foot suite, with a dressing room and walk-in closet that lead into the master bedroom.

Charm Reclaimed

The 1906 Tudor purchased by a Minneapolis couple, Karen and Steve Sonnenberg, needed work. So, with the help of the local design team of Gabriel Keller and Lars Peterssen, of Domain Architects, the Sonnenbergs set their goals. First, rectify a garish 1980s modernization of the 5,000-square-foot, three-story home. Particularly troubling was the 200-square-foot master bathroom, which had been stripped of original details and outfitted with a plum-colored tub, toilet, and sink. With their architects' help, Karen and Steve reestablished the room's vintage look and created a showcase for their Asian antiques collection. They also added modern conveniences, including a 50-square-foot dressing area and closet, and increased their storage and counter space.

The remodeling also allowed the couple to introduce elegant materials. The shower is outfitted with white ceramic subway tiles accented with mosaic borders of tumbled travertine, and the knotty-alder vanity is topped with tumbled pink marble that also forms its backsplash. Separate compartments for the toilet and stall shower create zones within the space and increase efficiency in a shared bath. At the same time, repetitive architectural elements like the transoms that top these compartments (as well as the new closet) help unify the space and keep it airy.

ABOVE: A new walk-in closet was built at the far end of the revamped bath. Warm, camel-colored walls pick up tones in the Oriental rug, the window treatment (made from an Indian sari), the gilt-framed mirror, and the wood vanity. The new freestanding clawfoot tub is fitted with a classic-style bath mixer and hand shower.

Before

ABOVE: A plum-colored pedestal sink and 1980s casement windows were jarring elements in this historic house.

RIGHT: A small closet in the master bedroom was gutted, plumbed, and attached to the bathroom as a separate toilet zone. It features a brick chimney wall uncovered during the renovation. Orb-shaped pendants from India illuminate the space and add a decorative touch. A fixed transom mimics movable ones elsewhere in the bath. BOTTOM: A roomy shower with a clear-glass door and a fixed, windowlike panel is located directly across from the toilet. The handsome trim work within the shower stall, is water-resistant solid surfacing.

The Wish List

- Reorder the space to make room for a large master closet
- Absorb a small existing closet into a separate toilet zone
- Install a double vanity
- Put in transoms above the closet, toilet, and shower to unify the look
- Add a separate 30-square-foot shower complete with bench

ABOVE: In the new plan, placing the clawfoot tub next to the window made room for a 7½-foot-long double vanity. A closet was added at one end of the room, while an old toilet area became a 5-by-6-foot shower.

Super Space-Saver

When architect Charles Schwartzapfel bought a two-bedroom apartment in a century-old building in New York City, he immediately made it his own—not by altering or expanding any spaces but by removing the remnants of its recent history. "The horrible wood paneling came off, and the dropped ceilings were removed," said Rachael Judge, a designer with Charles's firm, CRS Designs, Inc., in New York City. "Basically, everything that made the place feel small and closed-in came out so we could make it brighter, lighter, and much more functional. Our challenge was getting rid of the junk."

In renovating the apartment's only bathroom, the first step in the process was removing old brown ceramic tile and pulling out forty-year-old plumbing fixtures. The bathroom dimensions—little more than 5 by 8 feet—were essentially unchanged, and new fixtures were installed pretty much where the old ones had been. The difference is that the new elements are more functional, efficient, and attractive, and the space itself no longer feels dark and claustrophobic. White dominates; it appears on the vanity top, undermount sink, toilet, painted ceiling, and upper walls. The lower walls and floor are Portuguese limestone in a pale creamy white, with gray undertones; the trim is a rich gray-blue French limestone.

"We started with 16-inch tiles and had them cut," Judge recalled. The walls are covered with 8-by-16-inch tiles set in a staggered, bricklike pattern. There are 8-by-16 trim tiles just above the floor and 4-by-16 gray-

ABOVE, LEFT: Mirrors over the sink and behind each shelving niche reflect light and visually expand the space. ABOVE: A wall-mounted faucet conserves space on the sink deck. The vanity contains one open shelf and below it two 12-inch-square drawers for bath supplies. "I didn't want the clutter of cabinet doors that could make the room seem overbearing," Charles explained.

OPPOSITE: Smoothing out the perimeter of the compact bathroom was key to creating the illusion of spaciousness. Two examples of this strategy in action are recessed shelves and a low-profile toilet that extends partway into a wall cavity.

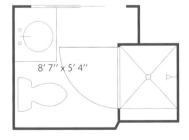

ABOVE: Several inches of open space above the toilet tank not only allow access for maintenance but stretch the room's storage capacity. Tucking that fixture into the wall saves floor space.

ABOVE, RIGHT: Hinged on the left, a frameless clear-glass door shields the room from water splashing out of the shower. Multiple showerheads, including body sprays and a hand-held spout, give the unit spalike elegance. A thermostat keeps the water temperature constant, and three volume controls determine which sprays are operational.

8' 7" x 5' 4"

ABOVE: Architect Schwartzapfel simplified his bathroom, eliminating obtrusive details and integrating storage into the space—all without expanding the size of the existing room.

blue tiles capping the creamy white limestone and extending around the room. A subtle detail that ties all the elements together is the satin-nickel wainscot edging that wraps the whole room. Charles explained that the edging was perforated "to allow the stone to read through."

The same two tones of limestone were used on the floor. Within a gray-blue border are 6-by-6-inch tiles cut down from the original 16-inch limestone squares and set at a 45-degree angle. The look, said Judge, "is almost like that of a carpet."

Overall, the room is spare, with open shelves in the vanity for towels and below them a pair of 12-inch drawers for bath supplies. Set into the walls are two storage niches. Both openings are mirror-backed; their reflections add to the volume of light in the space, making it feel more open, less confined. The niche beside the toilet had been a boarded-up window.

For unity and simplicity, the same materials are repeated throughout the room: clear glass on the shelving and shower door, satin-finish nickel on fittings and hardware, walnut on the base of the vanity and the frame surrounding the wall mirror. "Within a very small space, I wanted to give myself the opportunity, to enjoy the same luxury and simplicity I give my clients," said Charles. "As the design is clean and fluid, the room actually feels bigger than it is."

ABOVE: The open shower area features a bench, porcelain wall tiles, a slate floor, and a decorative 1-inch-square slate tile arched design. Beside the shower, a new private toilet was installed featuring a window with a view. ABOVE, RIGHT: The 36-inch-tall vanity, set into an alcove, was designed with plenty of built-in storage. The mirror's arched shape and frame, made of 1-inch slate tiles, repeats the arch motif in the adjacent shower stall. Terra-cotta walls, mosaic tile trim, and oiled bronze fixtures add to the warm Southwestern decor. BELOW: What had once been a narrow hallway leading to the backyard is now utilized as part of a new guest bath.

Before

Expanding in Style

After living in their house for twenty-five years and raising five children, now grown, Becky and Jim Hughes had no plans to move out of their spacious one-story 1960s home in Portland, Oregon. But they were aware that staying on would require changes to make their lives more comfortable.

Among the spaces they wanted to be reconfigured was a cramped lower-level bathroom, formerly the kids' bath, located past a storage room at the end of a long hall. The bath had a tiny corner shower, unattractive fixtures, little storage, peeling wallpaper, and a badly scuffed vinyl floor.

"We really wanted to eliminate that narrow, dark hallway and at the same time increase the size of the bathroom," says Becky, who was eager to turn this graceless space into a more spacious and inviting guest bath. To help them with the redesign, the couple called in builder Scott Gregor and designer Marlene Buckner, allied ASID, both of Master Plan Remodeling Design/Build in Portland.

Living in the cool, damp Northwest climate, Becky and Jim were attracted to Southwestern style as a way to create a warmer environment. They were also in need of more space, a more private toilet area, taller counters, and fixtures that would be comfortable for adults who had chosen to age in place. And Jim had a special request—a sauna.

To fulfill their list of demands, Gregor enlarged the bathroom by combining it with the storage room and part of the long hallway. Then he

Before

ABOVE: The old vanity with its worn laminate counter was squeezed into a corner between the door and the cramped shower. An opaque pane of yellow bull's-eye glass installed for privacy also shut out the view. BELOW: A bronze-toned wall sconce with a white shade adds a touch of classic elegance.

created a color scheme of terra-cotta, mustard-yellow, and a mix of two types of tiles—terra-cotta porcelain and apricot slate. For added texture and pattern, the tiles were cut into five different sizes and used on numerous surfaces and in various arrangements. To address the Hughes's aging-adult issues, doorways were designed without thresholds to trip over.

For ease of use, the maple vanity cabinet is 36 inches high, and the toilet, in its relocated private space, is a taller-than-normal model. "The shower space was also expanded," said Gregor. "Instead of installing shower doors, we added a shallow curb to keep water inside." Enjoying the new look, expanded space, and improved amenities, the homeowners are hard-pressed to recall the dreary, confined space that was once a neglected bath.

Color Tip

"Strong Southwestern colors set this room's theme," said Gregor. "We could create an entirely different look simply by changing colors."

The Wish List

- Double the size of the bath by stealing space from an adjoining storage room and a section of hallway
- Relocate the bathroom's entrance from the hallway into a new guest suite
- Add a 5-by-5-foot sauna
- Replace the old floor with slate flooring
- Create a private toilet area
- Install taller fixtures, allowing for more comfortable use

RIGHT: Formerly a kids' bath, the new guest bath now includes a vanity sink, open shower area, private toilet, and a sauna that can fit two people comfortably.

SHOWER   SAUNA

ABOVE: Wallpaper covered the walls and ceiling, making the old master bath appear small and claustrophobic. Matching tile on the vanity and shower stall only added to the cramped feeling. LEFT: The oversize shower takes up 30 square feet and features a clear-glass partition, double "rain forest" showerheads, and a built-in seat. Marble counters and rich wood cabinetry create a warm ambience, while the new window and skylight bring sunlight into the once-dingy room.

The Wish List

- Extend the bathroom area into the master bedroom
- Make room for an air-jet soaking tub
- Replace the old sink and vanity with new marble-topped South African anigre-wood storage cabinets and two vessel sinks
- Create a separate toilet room for privacy
- Move one of the windows to make room for a longer vanity
- Install a skylight
- Enlarge the shower stall so two people can use it
- Equip the oversize shower stall with double "rain forest" showerheads

Dated to Dazzling

Upon seeing the master bathroom of this 1980s contemporary home for the first time, the home buyers had a hard time envisioning the room's potential beneath the dated wallpaper that covered the ceiling and walls.

Jeffrey Glass, CEO of Construction Concepts in Stamford, Connecticut, was recruited to work with the couple on renovating their house. For the bath, he suggested expanding the room by annexing some space from the adjoining bedroom. In his new layout, Glass added a toilet room for privacy and a soaking tub, which sits beneath a skylight that brings light into the room via a 10-foot-tall tunnel. Walls and floor are honed marble tile that gives the room a spacious yet very relaxed feeling.

The location of a window was moved to make room for a new two-sink vanity, which features a marble top and South African anigre-wood cabinets. The large unit replaced the worn oak plywood cabinets and flashily tiled counter.

Room to Breathe

Having private his-and-hers bathrooms had always been a wonderful luxury for a St. Paul, Minnesota, couple, except for the fact that neither bath had been renovated for years—more than half a century, in fact. Finally concluding that improvements were needed, they called Lynn Monson, owner of DreamMaker Kitchen & Bath in St. Louis Park, Minnesota, to handle the task of overhauling both bathrooms. The tranquil, elegant bath featured here belongs to the wife.

At less than 55 square feet, the room's original dimensions were minuscule, making the space feel squeezed. It had old fixtures and finishes and lacked such modern-day comforts as a massage showerhead and a deep tub. Plus, the awkward layout had the toilet located behind the sink.

The DreamMaker crew began by removing an ungainly storage cabinet and swapping the locations of the sink and toilet. The introduction of natural surfaces—cherry and maple cabinets and limestone floor and wall tiles—along with a frosted-glass vanity, almost magically gave the room warmth and sophistication. A host of clever design strategies also ensure that the room looks spacious, despite its small size.

Take, for instance, the vanity. A custom-designed drawer appears to float at counter level suspended below a simple white above-counter sink. Flanking the sink are tall, narrow wall cabinets. As Monson explained, "We went vertical with the cabinets instead of having a big, old clunky vanity in the middle of the room. The cabinets offer a tremendous amount of storage and are at a better height ergonomically." Using the dark-colored limestone below and a light shade on the walls above draws the eye upward, making the room seem larger.

The designers agreed on a plan that would create a fresh, modern space that radiates unmistakable warmth. The result, when the remodeling concluded, was a soothing, comfortable room that looks and feels good.

Small-Space Tip

Use dark colors on the lower half of a room and lighter colors higher up. This will draw the eye upward and make a room appear larger than it really is.

Before

ABOVE: Poor lighting, a cramped layout, and dated fixtures added up to an uninviting and extremely uncomfortable bathroom.

ABOVE: Quality lighting and large mirrors combined with a frosted-glass wall-mounted counter, which appears to float, make this compact space look larger. The soft yellow wall tone enhances the tranquil feel of the room. LEFT: Except for changing locations of the sink and toilet, the designer retained the original layout of the bathroom

The Wish List

- Switch locations where the sink and toilet were placed
- Create a "floating" frosted-glass vanity drawer to make the small room appear larger
- Replace the old floor and walls with limestone tile

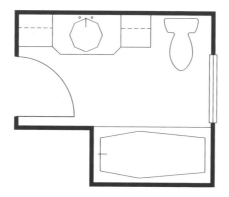

Aging in Comfort

With an older parent moving in, a West Coast couple concluded that they needed to convert their guest bath into a space that was welcoming, attractive and, most important of all, accessible. "They especially wanted to avoid the institutional look you would find in a nursing home," said interior designer Lisa Sten, of Harrell Remodeling in Mountain View, California.

To complete an efficient, barrier-free design, Sten needed additional square footage that would accommodate a wider doorway, so she moved a wall 2 feet into an adjacent bedroom. She then installed helpful features, such as 36-inch-wide pocket doors to create an extra-wide entry and a curbless shower with grab bars and a fold-down bench.

"For the shower floor, we decided to use 1-inch slip-resistant porcelain tiles in a soothing sage-green," Sten explained. "Although small tiles mean more grout lines—and a bigger cleanup job—they provide the traction needed to reduce the chance of slipping in a wet area."

With the bathroom's functional upgrades realized, the designer set her sights on improving the look of the space. Overall, a well-balanced mix of materials—honed granite, tempered glass, and weathered metal—give the room an earthy elegance. Serving as a focal point is a handsome new granite-topped vanity resting on a wrought-iron base. The piece adds a decorative touch while visually expanding the 70-square-foot space.

On the walls, a celadon-green tile border positioned at chair-rail height plus contrasting stamp-size accent tiles in the shower add dollops of color to the mostly neutral palette. "It's a beautiful bath," Sten exclaimed. "You'd have to look really hard to find the modifications."

ABOVE: To gain additional square footage, the bathtub was removed and replaced with an open shower area designed to blend into the space.

Before

ABOVE: Although the old bath had acceptable standard fixtures, the owners knew it wouldn't work for anyone with special needs. OPPOSITE: Designer Sten eliminated a vanity and replaced it with a sink and wrought-iron base. A larger window was placed on the shower wall, allowing natural light to flood the room.

Before

ABOVE: This narrow hall bath required renovation to suit a senior citizen. Since the bathtub would go unused, it was removed in favor of a curbless shower.

After

ABOVE: Enlarging the bath meant providing additional space for such modifications as a wider doorway, wheelchair-turnaround clearance, and a spacious open shower.

The Wish List

- Gain 20 square feet by appropriating 2 feet from the adjoining bedroom
- Enlarge doorway with 36-inch-wide pocket doors
- Install a wheelchair-accessible curbless shower with slip-resistant floor tiles
- Remove the old sink and replace it with a granite-topped vanity
- Put in a taller 16-inch-high toilet, as opposed to a standard 15-inch one.

Zen-like Sensibility

Designer Kelly Vogan was faced with a challenge: open up a dark, narrow, basement-level master bath without making it wider or adding windows. The bath was compartmentalized and felt confined, its shower stall and toilet separated from the vanity area by a wall. "Our plan was mainly to unify the space," explained Vogan, head of the design/build firm Vogan Associates in Silver Spring, Maryland.

To achieve this goal, Vogan's team, including the architect George Graupera, followed three basic remodeling rules: go up, borrow inches from another room, and remove interior walls.

First, Vogan demolished and removed the walled-in shower and toilet area from the 6-by-14-foot space, then raised the ceiling 4 inches to make the room feel more open. The new shower, now placed at the rear of the room, is made of glass that appears to rise out of the floor, which in fact it does. "When we poured the concrete slab floor, we cut a slot and anchored the glass," Vogan recalled. A hinged glass door swings open to allow entry.

Instead of a traditional look, the homeowners decided to add a little Asian flair. Authentic shaved river rock, embedded into the gently sloping floor, runs straight into the glass-enclosed shower without being interrupted by a lip. "We wanted a soothing, yet exotic ambience," said one of the homeowners. A freestanding Far Eastern-style armoire placed into a 3-by-30-inch niche—borrowed from an adjacent room—serves as an aesthetic focal point and a place to stow bath essentials.

For additional storage, a dark stained-wood vanity with drawers and undersink space was designed to extend the length of one wall. The wide marble top allows for substantial counter space and accommodates two users at one time comfortably. Tilted mirrors and backsplash-mounted faucets—easier to clean than deck-mounted models—add a sleek look.

Lastly, Vogan tackled the problem of the door. A standard swing-in style would invariably be in the way and always take up precious room, so he selected and installed a custom pocket door that slides open and shut and has elegant divided-light frosted glass. He also directed considerable attention to adding decorative details. As Vogan explained, "The homeowners were looking for an alternative to wood trim around the door, so we decided to go with a plaster trim for the door as well as the ceiling."

Now a far cry from its earlier configuration, this master bath's overall contemporary look has proved to be highly relaxing and contemplative—as soothing, in fact, as a Zen retreat.

Before

ABOVE: Located in the basement, the old bath was a narrow, dark space divided by compartments and devoid of windows.

BELOW: This custom pocket door is less intrusive than the previous swinging door. Tilted mirrors, wall-mounted faucets, and a specially designed vanity add significant details.

The Wish List

- Raise the ceiling 4 inches
- Replace a standard shower-stall frame with an all-glass enclosure
- Add a custom vanity to provide extra storage
- Carve out a niche in the wall to hold an armoire
- Install river-rock flooring

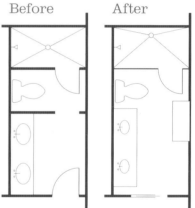

Before   After

ABOVE, LEFT: A wall separating the vanities from the toilet created a closed-in feeling in the original narrow bath. ABOVE, RIGHT: To visually open the space, the walls were removed, a glass-enclosed shower was installed, and the conventional swing-open door was replaced with a pocket door.

ABOVE: In addition to including a custom-made vanity, Vogan added storage space by tucking an armoire into a niche in one wall. On the open bottom shelf, fluffy white towels are close at hand.

Storage Tip

When remodeling a room, check to see if it is possible to steal extra square footage from an adjoining space.

Two at Once

When Karen and Brian Colautti-Pine purchased their 1917 house in the Riverdale neighborhood of Toronto, they were drawn to its charm. "It's kind of a cross between Victorian and Craftsman styles," Karen believed. But the three-bedroom, three-bath home also had problems. "At one point it was a boarding house," she reported. "It had been renovated poorly at various times and was in pretty bad shape when we bought it." Since then, however, the couple has slowly transformed it by making budget-smart improvements, room by room.

Among their most notable redos are the master bathroom and powder room. "When we finally decided what to do with the kitchen, we figured we should also redo the upstairs master bathroom and the guest bath directly below it," said Karen. The couple saved time and footwork by doing everything at once—and also negotiated price deals on the plumbing supplies they needed. And since Karen and Brian were not only determined home improvers but talented craftspeople as well, they did the entire renovation themselves over a five- month period.

The 7-by-10-foot master bath upstairs was the first to be gutted. The couple peeled off the decaying remnants of previous renovations, then carefully removed the sink, toilet, and porcelain tub, which were all in good enough condition to keep. Next, they ripped out worn wall tile, which left some gaps in the walls. They also tore off layers of old floor tile and linoleum until reaching the original wood subfloor.

Stripped to the bones, the space was ready for its makeover. The couple began by patching the holes, adding insulation, and covering the walls with white beadboard. For a timeless look, Karen chose black-and-white mosaic tiles for the floor, which she and Brian set in a classic diamond pattern. "When we bought the house, the sink and toilet in the master bath were squeezed in under the window," Karen recalled.

Before

ABOVE: While renovating the master bath, Brian and Karen left the tub where it was, but installed new tile above and around it, and added new shower fittings. They removed the old tile, which covered the floor and ran three-quarters of the way up the walls. The sink and toilet were moved from under the window to the adjacent wall. BELOW: In the remodeled master bath, a wooden medicine cabinet from the downstairs bath was added and perked up with white paint. Sunlight filters through the curtain that dresses the original window. White fixtures, a white-painted towel rack and shelf, plus the repainted medicine cabinet create a vintage look, set against the bead-board walls.

What They Loved

- The size of the bath and its convenient location
- The window and old plumbing fixtures
- The potential for creating order and charm where none previously existed

What They Hated

- An unworkable layout, with poorly arranged fixtures
- Ugly old tile walls and flooring
- A gloomy color scheme that was neither pleasant nor inviting

What They Loved

- The first-floor location of the bathroom
- The possibility of reusing the existing toilet
- Floor tile in good enough condition to be reinstalled in the laundry room

What They Hated

- A clumsy arrangement of shower, sink and toilet
- The corner shower, which wasn't needed in a powder room
- More square footage than the room needed

The couple spaced out these fixtures more sensibly against the wall opposite the tub. They also retained the room's original window but crafted new window-casing millwork as well as baseboard molding. Finally, they placed a new shower over the tub, put up a crisp white shower curtain, and hung a ready-made window curtain in front of the window.

For Karen and Brian, one of the house's main attractions was its conveniently placed first-floor powder room. "It was once a pantry," said Karen. Since there were no bedrooms on that level, its shower seemed superfluous, so the couple eliminated it, shrinking the bath to 4-by-6 feet and adding bonus square footage to their kitchen remodel. In gutting the bath, they removed its 12-by-12-inch floor tiles carefully, then reused them in the laundry room. The room's small existing window needed replacement. "But as we didn't want to have to replace the header," Karen explained, "we put in a new frosted-glass window that was the same size."

Another budget-smart step the couple took to improve the powder room was to install the same flooring that they used for the kitchen. "It's a laminate that looks like an old wooden barn floor," she explained. Also, as in the master bath, she and Brian crafted the window casing and baseboard molding—and even built a combination shelf and dowel directly above a new toile tieback curtain. Although the couple purchased a new pedestal sink, mirror, shelf, and sconces, they recycled and repositioned the original toilet. Throughout both baths, new faucets and handles freshened up all of the recycled fixtures.

Living with gutted-out spaces for several months—and trekking down to the basement bathroom to wash dishes and bathe—proved worthwhile, in light of what Karen and Brian achieved. "I have really expensive taste," Karen confided. "I just don't want to have to pay for it."

ABOVE: For the powder room, Karen sewed loops and fringe on a curtain panel, then swagged it for dramatic effect. She positioned it to emphasize the height of the room and make the window appear larger. An old glass doorknob was mounted on the wall so the powder room curtain could tie back with black cording to the knob. BELOW: The old downstairs bath had a corner shower and a vanity that were no longer needed. Both were scrapped; only the toilet, of fairly recent vintage, was reused.

Before

Before

LEFT: The height of subway tiles rises to the middle line of the window to reduce visual clutter. The Carrara marble used on the tub ledge and backsplash is also on the vanity countertop. ABOVE: Before the bath was remodelled, an off-center window and an obtrusive radiator posed puzzling layout problems.

Reordered Elements

After buying their circa-1895 home, a Montclair, New Jersey, couple decided to postpone remodeling the troubled second bathroom, as more pressing needs—furnace replacement, for one—were looming. They lived with the bathroom's leaks until it became a major problem. That's when they asked interior designer Tracey Stephens, also of Montclair, to help design a new bath. Stephens had worked with the couple before, doing several whole-house renovations, and they liked her work.

At the time of the renovation, the homeowners' two children were young and still taking tub baths. "The goal was to have a generously sized tub that both kids could bathe in," Stephens recalled. They chose a roomy 6-foot-long whirlpool framed by a deep ledge. But the 7-by-9-foot room created a dilemma. Stephens considered a few different arrangements of tub, toilet, and sink until she decided that placing the tub under the window looked and felt right. Because the homeowners had a stall shower in the master bath, they were willing to forgo a shower in this one. The old window was replaced by a larger double-hung unit to let more natural light into the room. Frosted glass was placed in the lower part of the window for privacy.

The Wish List

- Change the tub location from the left of the entry to the back wall of the room
- Replace the old radiator, an eyesore under the window, with a recessed model mounted beside the door
- Order a freestanding custom vanity to get the most possible storage for the space (a hallway linen closet holds the towels)
- Install a dark-stained white-oak floor treated with a tung-oil finish
- Remove a swing-door entry in favor of a pocket door to liberate space
- Illuminate the bath with four polished-chrome sconces controlled by dimmers

Top Tip

Working with white requires textural interest to add dimension. Designer Stephens suggested coordinating different textures and blending in shades of white. Here, she used 3-by-6-inch subway tiles, Carrara marble, and white-painted bead board.

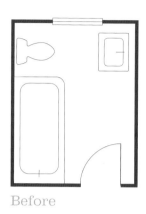

Before

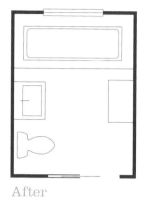

After

FAR LEFT: The original bath had a standard layout. LEFT: A much larger whirlpool tub now sits in front of the window. Located on opposite walls, the pedestal sink and freestanding custom vanity face each other. By substituting a pocket door, Stephens was able to nestle the toilet in the corner next to the sink. BELOW, LEFT: Towels hang within reach on a double towel rack of polished chrome and clear-glass bars. BELOW, RIGHT: A recessed open-shelf unit flanked by two chrome sconces is hung directly over a custom vanity.

Before

ABOVE: Patterned wallpaper and dingy aqua tile gave this bath a worn and dated look. The vintage toilet had to be replaced, but the homeowners kept the recently purchased pedestal sink. LEFT: Soft-blue walls, crisp white bead-board paneling, blue and white accessories, and off-white tiles create a relaxing ambience in this remodeled bathroom.

Revived With Color
After their older son left home for college, the owners of this century-old house decided to turn his bath into a much-needed guest bathroom. Inspired by a clutch of ideas collected from home-decorating magazines, the couple decided on a soft color palette—mostly white with just a hint of blue—and a mix of vintage and contemporary styles.

They took their ideas to a local home center and gathered ceramic tile samples, paint chips, and information on plumbing. Learning from past lighting mistakes, they decided to consult an in-store designer who

The Wish List
- Replace the tub with a new stall shower
- Remove wall tile and replace it with 40-inch-tall bead-board paneling
- Eliminate a second doorway to gain more wall space
- Replace the old toilet
- Update the linen closet with shutter doors
- Add simple new lighting

helped them select a combination of recessed lights and a decorative fixture.

Since all of the plumbing was already in place, the room wouldn't require major changes, except for replacing the rarely used tub with a shower stall, which turned out to be more complicated than anticipated. A standard shower stall should have a length and width of at least 36 inches, but this bath had only 31 inches available in either direction. The homeowners consulted a contractor who urged them to install a custom shower unit. By positioning the stall at an angle, the contractor was able to accommodate the 36-by-36-inch dimension that was needed for comfort.

The room also had a built-in floor-to-ceiling cabinet, so no additional storage space was needed. What the room did need, however, was more wall space, which was achieved by eliminating a second doorway.

When the owners' son returned home from college for a visit, he could hardly recognize his old bathroom. Like him, the room was all grown up.

Before

Before

TOP: The homeowners kept the existing spacious floor-to-ceiling closet but changed its look by replacing unattractive old doors. ABOVE: A pair of 31-by-72-inch plantation shutters replaced the original closet doors. The slats in the doors can open to allow air to circulate. LEFT: The rarely used tub, framed by drab tiles, was once truly an eyesore. FAR LEFT: The old cast-iron tub was replaced by a tiled shower stall. A 25-inch chrome-and-glass shower door was selected to match the fixtures.

Ingenious Storage

Where storage issues are concerned, particularly in bathrooms, necessity is undoubtedly the mother of invention. If every bathroom had the space to fulfill every possible storage need, few designers would ever feel challenged. As it is, however, relatively few homeowners can boast that, without pondering the question at great length and harnessing every ounce of ingenuity, they have more than enough space for all their bathroom gear.

Although pedestal sinks have grace and style, they find greater acceptance in powder rooms or guest baths where demand for backup supplies is minimal. For heavy-use baths, particularly master bathrooms, vanities are the usual choice. But even they have limitations: even if there is only one sink, plumbing pipes take up what might otherwise be drawer or shelf space. Perhaps this is why vessel sinks have achieved such prominence. They add sculptural shape and often needed contrast; they also sit on top of vanities, rather than down inside, which means there is more usable space directly below the countertops.

To eliminate clutter, or that often unavoidable feeling of claustrophobia, some designers prefer to shift storage needs out of the bath and into a nearby linen closet or a hall cabinet located near the bathroom door. Choices are made individually—whatever makes a homeowner happy. In addition to ideas pictured on these pages, consider the following:

- Niches cut into walls (between studs), behind a tub or shower, for soaps and shampoos
- Triangular or wedge-shaped shelving located in otherwise empty corners
- Drawer dividers sized specifically to hold grooming needs and a hair dryer
- An expanded medicine cabinet with shelves deep enough to hold all medications Assess your needs before taking any action. Bath storage is challenging but not impossible.

ABOVE: To stretch storage space without adding bulky furniture to a small bathroom, clean folded towels can be stacked on a room-wide shelf that is mounted high on a wall, up near the ceiling.

LEFT: The toilet compartment in this bath includes a niche set into the wall to hold reading matter.

ABOVE: In a two-person bath, a tall cherry cabinet does triple duty, separating the his and hers zones, holding all of a couple's grooming supplies, and adding striking contrast to the decor.

LEFT: This vanity is smart and attractive, but the most remarkable enhancement may be its color. Light gray cabinets with a white top give the illusion of much more space than actually exists. A super-wide countertop provides room for applying makeup. BELOW: Generous towel storage is a key element in a bath utilized most frequently by three young adults. In fashioning the vanity's finest detail, designer Tony Hunt, of Pickering, Ontario, eliminated two drawers and replaced a third with pull-out towel bars. .

RIGHT: Storage cubbies at the foot of this tub keep towels and soaps dry but close at hand.

OPPOSITE; ABOVE, LEFT: Roll-out wire baskets keep towels and other bathroom essentials neatly tucked away yet easily accessible. OPPOSITE; ABOVE, RIGHT: This cleverly contoured drawer interior rescues the dead space typically lost to the dip of the wash basin. OPPOSITE; BELOW, LEFT: Privacy walls can do much more than hide a toilet. The trapezoid-shaped opening in this wall admits light from the windows behind the toilet. Glass shelves provide storage and display space and, as a special finishing touch, decorative molding frames the opening. OPPOSITE; BELOW, RIGHT: A multilevel privacy wall adds a sculptural element to this bath. Nooks are used for storage and display, but there is room for a spot to mount a towel hook.

PART 4

Design Is in the Details

The whole is greater than the sum of its parts. We absorbed that lesson in high school, probably in a physics class, but it is relevant in nearly every context, particularly when it comes to decorating, redecorating, or remodeling all or part of a home. For example, you can replace the hardware on kitchen cabinets, repaint the walls of your bedroom, or add a porch to the front or back of your house. But no matter what you do, whether a major or modest undertaking, it cannot be considered in isolation. New hardware may introduce a style that either muddles the look of your kitchen or takes it to a new dimension. The look of fresh paint in a bedroom, unless you repeat the same old color, will affect every area that leads to that room. And a new porch will surely impact your home's front or rear elevation, blending in and improving the facade or simply blighting it—there is always that risk.

Vern Yip, an architectural interior designer featured on cable TV's Fine Living Network, once proclaimed that changing the look of a home is, first of all, "not about decorating; it's about having a purposeful space plan. It's also about understanding scale in that space." The way he treats rooms, he explained, "depends on how much time people plan to spend there."

Clodagh, a renowned interior designer, declared, "It's not what you use but how you use it—the juxtaposition of materials." Her point suggests a subtlety often absent from decorating. The heavy earth tones she favors are punctuated by tactile contrasts, sometimes dramatic enough to make you stop in your tracks. In a home, she said, "everywhere you look, everywhere you walk, you should see something beautiful."

Color is important, of course, whether you are selecting wall tones or fabric patterns. In the right light, dramatic colors can draw people into a space (understanding color also means understanding light). Is color ever an impediment? It shouldn't be. Take the time and effort to pick colors that fill the space and make you feel good about your choices. Color trends are for marketers. You can do no better than to surround yourself with the colors that please you, the ones you know you enjoy living with. What about family and friends? Said California architect Douglas Burge: "I always say that if it's done right, anyone who appreciates design should appreciate it."

OPPOSITE: Texture and tone add interest to this fireplace wall when slate tiles in various sizes and tones are applied. A contrasting dark slate surrounds the actual gas-log-burning firebox.

Upward Action

Crowded for too long into a shoe-box-size bedroom on the first floor of their home, Jeff Wong and Valérie Bonvin decided to convert the partially finished attic of their 1,500-square-foot bungalow in Portland, Oregon, into a spacious master suite. Because much of the ductwork and electrical wiring were already in place, the homeowners decided to tackle the project themselves, with Jeff assuming the role of general contractor. However, the plumbing, plastering, and framing parts of the remodel were naturally deferred to professionals.

Having spent seven years restoring their circa-1926 home, Jeff and Valérie were already remodeling veterans when they decided to give their attic space a modern loftlike edge. Hoping to find unusual materials that would work within the loft context, the couple searched for salvaged items to incorporate into the space. For instance, Jeff rescued siding from a late-19th-century barn that was being razed. Then he purchased random-length fir-plank flooring from a salvage yard. That weathered wood, compatible with flooring in downstairs rooms, visually links the two areas.

OPPOSITE, LEFT: The biggest challenge in converting the dark, unused attic to living space was providing privacy for the bath while remaining faithful to the open-loft concept. (A partial wall built at one end of the room would solve that problem.) ABOVE: When all the work was done, the couple agreed on a pared-down aesthetic, insisting that the space remain spare and open. Not visible here because tucked under the eaves, is roll-out pantry-style shelving that functions as closet storage.

RIGHT: A partial wall separates bedroom and bath areas. A restrained color palette defines this bath as a sophisticated, soothing retreat. BELOW, RIGHT: At the top of the stairs, rough siding salvaged from a century-old barn is juxtaposed with a stainless steel guardrail that Jeff designed.

The Wish List

- Convert the walk-up attic space into a 525-square-foot master suite
- Install three skylights
- Replace the old floor with reclaimed random-length fir planking
- Build a partial wall separating bedroom from bathroom
- Panel one attic wall with recycled barn siding
- Install stainless steel-cable guardrails
- Create storage under the eaves
- Add cable lighting and hollow wood beams overhead

Before

Problem A small attic room had become a catchall for seasonal or rarely used items. Meanwhile, the owner did her paperwork at a cramped kitchen desk and craft projects landed on the dining room table. Supplies and records were stashed haphazardly throughout the house.

Solution The first step was serious uncluttering—getting rid of everything that was saved for those "just in case" moments and moving the rest to the garage. Next, the room was measured and plans were made to divide the space into a desk area and a crafting station. To make the most of whatever storage space remained, white cabinets and shelves were used liberally throughout to maintain an airy, open look and also minimize clutter. The mix of open and closed storage gave the owner access to all those items she uses most often—but without ever creating a mess.

ABOVE: In the attic's craft corner, framed painted pegboard becomes an attractive, practical addition to storage drawers and shelving. It also keeps high-use essentials visible. LEFT: Bare windows that let in natural light plus a cheery shade of turquoise paint on the walls makes this a bright, inviting space. The white ceiling visually raises the sloping roof, and wall-to-wall carpeting not only unifies the space but also makes it seem larger. The desk was fashioned by topping two small cabinets with a 6-foot-long counter. RIGHT: Before the renovation, the attic space, though a sunny spot, was a catchall for household clutter.

ABOVE, LEFT: A two-shelf stacking unit from a closet shop helps keep the desktop clear of paperwork, reference books, and stationery. ABOVE: A framed sheet of corkboard hung on the wall behind the desk combines business with pleasure—snapshots, artwork, invitations, business cards, and memos give the desk area a homey, personal look. BELOW: Under the eaves, a corner that's too small for furniture yet too big to waste proves the perfect spot for extra storage. Here, adjustable wall-mounted shelves hold clearly labeled boxes of supplies.

ABOVE: Color-coded folders make things easy to find and file and provide the inspiration for the whimsical striped border on the desk chair. Kitchen-drawer organizers were used to contain the items stowed in the top drawers.

Color Squares

Here's an easy craft project that will yield color accents to perk up any room.

Tools and materials

- water-based paint
- metal straight-edge ruler
- pencil
- low-tack, 1-inch masking tape
- paintbrushes (2½-inch-wide, fine-tip)

1 Decide on what size squares you want for your border or to frame as wall art. Using a metal ruler and pencil, mark out the top and bottom of the squares, measuring up from the top of the baseboard.

2 Use the ruler to mark out the width of each square.

3 Use masking tape to define the top, bottom, and edges of each square.

4 Brush on the paint, allowing squares to dry before carefully removing the masking tape. If creating a border, apply more tape to define neighboring squares until the entire border is complete.

5 Allow new squares to dry thoroughly, then remove the masking tape. Use a fine-tipped paintbrush to touch up the edges of any square where the paint may appear uneven.

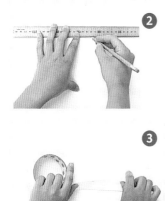

1

2

3

4

5

Basement Bonanza

When Eddy and Gail Yager of Vienna, Virginia, wanted to create a family room with organized storage and a home office in their 2,850-square-foot house, they decided to take advantage of the sizable space and roughed-in plumbing in their unfinished basement.

The challenge for Peggy and Ken Fisher, of the local design-build firm The Fisher Group, was to turn a raw space with many support columns and ductwork into a family center complete with an office, exercise rooms, a wet bar, a media room, and a new bathroom. "Fortunately, we had a creative HVAC contractor who managed to relocate a large amount of ductwork around a steel I-beam," the builder, Ken Fisher, recalls. "The space had high ceilings throughout, except for one area whose ceilings were low; that's where we located the exercise room and the office."

At the client's request, Peggy Fisher, the interior designer, created multiple rooms decorated in muted, earthy colors and finished off with furnishings that reflect the Arts and Crafts movement. In planning the area, she also paid attention to a special request for extra storage space.

"As it turned out," she said, "the stairwell, which we thought would be one of the drawbacks of the space, turned into a perfect spot to display some of the Yagers' race-car memorabilia."

ABOVE: Originally, the stairwell, which came down through the middle of the space at a near 45-degree angle, was a challenge since it ended near an awkwardly placed column. BELOW, LEFT: A wall of built-in cabinets in quarter-sawn white oak contains the media center and sound system to keep the room uncluttered. The comfortable new furniture is almost a signature of the Arts and Crafts style, as is the area's earthy palette.

The Wish List

- Finish a basement to create a media room, play area, bathroom, home office, wet bar, and exercise room
- Wrap a significant amount of ductwork around a steel beam, then build walls, a ceiling, and soffits around existing ducts, steel beams, and columns
- Enlarge windows and lower windowsills to outside grade level
- Create a display area and equip the media room with a giant TV, sound system, and additional storage
- Install recessed lighting

PLAY ROOM

FURNITURE AND STORAGE AREA

MEDIA ROOM

OFFICE

FIREPLACE AREA

CEDAR CLOSET

PANTRY   BAR

BATH

EXERCISE ROOM

CL

After

TOP: The ceramic tile used in the steam shower also covers the floor and the walls surrounding the vanity, creating a soothing blend of color. The smaller pieces of tile trim accent both the vanity and the shower wall. TOP, RIGHT: Open space under the stairs was turned into a display zone for collectibles. ABOVE: An elegant Arts and Crafts-style mirror and wall sconces add finishing touches to the bathroom. As in the media center, open shelves provide storage, this time for towels.

ABOVE: Slate tiles in three tones cover the walls in a niche carved out for the wet bar and also appear on the fireplace wall (not shown). The ceramic tile on the counter is also used in the bathroom. ABOVE, CENTER: Walled-off rooms and open spaces make a raw basement a livable environment.

Down-Under Decorating

Thanks to creative storage solutions and goof-proof color choices, it's possible to transform a dark, disorganized basement into a functional, appealing gathering place for the whole family. Glossy as well as matte paint was the key to revitalizing this room affordably—its palette taken from one graduated color strip to achieve a coordinated look. Here are other ways to make finished basement space attractive:

• Add contrast coloring in an office area; keep important papers in yellow binders, to add zest to the scheme.

• For youngsters, a low-cost, ready-to-assemble table for drawing, or doing homework or craft projects, is a good choice.

• To help soften the stark lines of industrial shelving, periodically bring in cut flowers from the yard or buy a bunch from the supermarket.

ABOVE: Easily installed wainscotting from a home center was applied to basement walls and painted pure white to add visual interest. Industrial-style racks support skis and other sports equipment.

OPPOSITE; ABOVE, LEFT: Commercial metal shelving enlivened with a fresh coat of violet paint ties into the palette yet sets the unit apart from the paler walls. Utilitarian metal storage boxes keep oft-used items close at hand. Wicker baskets, another affordable storage device, add warmth and serve as catchalls for loose papers and oversize items. OPPOSITE; BELOW, LEFT: A stackable washer-dryer unit is the ideal solution when floor space is in short supply. Tall, open storage cubbies—for detergent, bleach, and other sundries—were painted white to unify and define the new laundry area; they succeed in adding balance and scale when placed alongside the towering appliances.

RIGHT: To create a more efficient home office, shelves were built from plywood mounted against a wood frame and painted to blend in with the color scheme. A counter-height table with a shelf for work in progress was tucked between the shelf unit's vertical supports. BELOW, RIGHT: To keep drawing table clutter easily under control, bands of color-coordinated storage boxes were arranged on wall-hung shelves adjacent to the table. An adjustable swing-arm lamp takes up no work space as it is clamped firmly to the very edge of the table.

Before

ABOVE: The old porch had fallen into disrepair, its floor rotted through. The porch entrance and front steps were located awkwardly to the right of the door. LEFT: The new porch has two levels; the upper section is accessible from the master bedroom. Paint perked up the house's facade.

History Revealed

Studying the facade of their house, the owners of this 1890s Victorian in Columbus, Ohio, had a feeling it was missing an architectural element and thought a new porch would fill the void. Steve Hurtt, of Urban Order Architecture in Columbus, was happy to tackle the job, but he also had a hunch. Certain the house's vinyl siding was hiding historic trim and molding, he convinced his clients to peel away the vinyl. Doing so revealed the original wood siding plus 19th-century details, including two sunburst designs applied just below the roof.

"It was very exciting, like finding buried treasure," said Hurtt. "Anything that was removed or destroyed over the years we were able to recreate from shadow lines." Besides adding a new porch, the owners decided to use paint to restore the house's original appearance. The project earned Hurtt's firm a 2004 Chrysalis award for best exterior facelift.

The Wish List

- Remove all the vinyl siding on the house's facade
- Raze original front porch
- Design and build a two-story porch and move the steps to align with the front door
- Provide custom mahogany doors for the main entrance and upstairs master bedroom
- Paint the house in colors consistent with its 19th-century heritage (blue, yellow, and white)

Asian Influence

Although a new entry wasn't planned, halfway through a major remodeling project, the owners of a 1960s California ranch-style home decided to add one to their job list. "They had spent a number of years in Japan and were influenced by its architecture and design," recalled Paul Winans, whose firm, Winans Construction in Oakland, won a 2002 Chrysalis Award for Best Exterior Facelift and a 2003 Coty for Residential Specialty for its Zen-like interpretation of a ranch-style vernacular. The new exterior incorporates many familiar tenets of Japanese design. A trellised entranceway and cedar fence define the inner courtyard, creating a buffer between the house and the outside world. A small boulder on the right side, positioned behind the trellis, injects a sculptural note. The textured pathway is designed to guide guests to a series of carefully orchestrated sensory cues—the sound of cascading water and the sensation of stone underfoot—before they reach the front door. "It was important that the entry convey a strong sense of place," said Winans, who made sure his clients' affinity for Asian design was evident throughout this setting.

Before

ABOVE: Before the renovation, the front yard lacked color and texture. Although the owners hadn't originally planned to redo the entry, they ultimately decided a bland 1960s-era exterior could never be a satisfactory lead-in to the interior renovation. BELOW: A well-edited mix of materials and textures gives the new entry Asian-style visual and tactile interest. Beyond the trellised entranceway and cedar fence, exposed aggregate and flagstone pavers enliven the new walkway. The dining room's bay window was replaced by French doors that open onto an outdoor eating area partly shielded by cedar fencing.

The Wish List

- Put in a new arbor, cedar fencing, and trelliswork
- Add a small outdoor sitting area off the dining room
- Install concrete bench seating and a water feature
- Redesign the walkway, using aggregate and flagstone
- Place new exterior lighting throughout the courtyard area

Sunroom Added

Sandy Adams Doyle of Lodge Forest, Maryland, had long felt that a house with a water view deserved more than an unprotected front deck. Sandy, who shares her waterfront Cape Cod-style home with her husband and two children, explained that "We had an existing deck we could use only minimally because of the hot sun and the bugs." In truth, she added, "The only eating that happened out on the deck was done by mosquitoes." Seeking a solution, the Doyles turned to NatureScape Sunrooms. "They have a lovely home and really wanted to design a sunroom that would help them take advantage of their water views," according to Mike Smith, the brand manager for NatureScape.

To help her design the right sunroom for her classic-style home, Sandy met with Wayne Brechtel, the owner of PG Awning of Glen Burnie, Maryland, a local NatureScape dealer and installer. "Sandy and her husband wanted something they could enjoy year-round," Brechtel recalled. The 12-by-20-foot sunroom he designed for them features a gabled roof and ten sets of sliding windows complete with glass panels below each window, and two French-style doors that offer unobstructed views. Sandy reported that the new indoor/outdoor space quickly became a central part of their home.

Before

TOP: The sunroom's bright white facade complements the home's existing blue-gray clapboard exterior. The new addition also features a shingle-style roof that matches the roof on the main house. ABOVE: Before the sunroom was designed and installed, stone steps and wood railings led up to an open deck that was eventually reinforced.

Before

ABOVE: The Doyles's old family room had two large windows and a single glass sliding door with square panes that interrupted the water view. The sliding door opened onto a small wooden deck that offered limited access to the backyard. LEFT: Inside the sunroom, two upholstered armchairs with matching ottomans create a perfect place for reading the morning paper or enjoying the water views. BELOW, LEFT: In the new plan, the steps and a portion of the existing deck were reused, but the deck itself would need reinforcement to support the weight of the new sunroom. BELOW: The room has windows on three sides, plus two sets of doors. Its framing has an insulating vinyl barrier; its windows and doors are made of energy-saving insulated vinyl with low-e glass and argon gas.

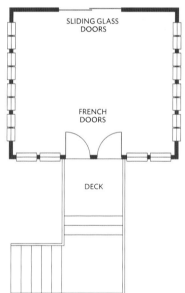

SLIDING GLASS DOORS

FRENCH DOORS

DECK

Top Tip
Sunrooms should complement a house's style. Choose a location with killer views, and don't skimp on windows.

REPLACE A PORCH LATTICE

Tools and materials
- flat pry bar • measuring tape
- drill driver • saber or circular saw (for cutting the lattice) • claw hammer •
reciprocating saw • 1-by-6-inch cedar or pressure-treated lumber (how much wood depends on your porch size) •
plastic or wood lattice (comes in 4-by-8-foot sheets) • paint primer • gloss enamel trim paint to match your porch
• 6-inch mending plates • flat corner braces • T-plates • 1-inch panhead screws and washers • $3/4$-inch screws
• 3- or 4-inch strap or T-hinges (two hinges are fine for a panel 8 feet or shorter, but use three hinges on one longer than 8 feet)

1 Remove the old lattice skirt with a flat pry bar. If necessary, cut into pieces with a reciprocating saw. Measure the openings between columns or posts. The completed frames should be $1/2$ inch narrower than the overall width and 1 inch shorter than the height.

2 Make the four perimeter pieces of each frame out of 1-by-6-inch lumber cut to a length of $4^{1}/_{2}$ feet. Be sure to choose a 1 by 4 for the center stile. Hold each corner joint of the frame together by using a 6-inch mending plate and a flat corner brace.

3 Cut the frame parts to length and assemble them face down on a flat surface. Use two T-plates to secure the 1-by-4 center stile to the frame. Position the hardware pieces about $1/4$ inch from the edge of the frame, and secure them with $3/4$-inch flathead screws.

4 Begin by cutting the lattice panels down to size. Lay the frames face down and attach the lattice with 1-inch panhead screws driven through washers. Screw the lattice to the back of the frames after drilling oversize clearance holes.

5 Drill clearance holes that are slightly larger than the screw shanks so the lattice can expand and contract without buckling as the weather changes. If a frame has a center stile, secure the seam between the pieces of lattice with two rows of screws.

6 Hang the framed lattice panels from the porch with either 3- or 4-inch strap or T-hinges. Screw the hinges to the frames first, then set the panels in the openings under the porch. Slip a pry bar under the panel and raise it up tight against the porch front.

MAKE A WATERFALL

Tools and materials
• flexible vinyl tubing • 4 to 8 large flat slate stones • a Beckett Fountain Kit • small rocks • metal grate • carpenter's level • plastic bin • ground fault circuit interrupter

1 Follow instructions on fountain kit to build a metal-grate ground base for your fountain. Stack rocks over it to form a flat surface, then top it all off with large slate stones set in a cascading pattern.

2 Place the end of the vinyl tubing at the top of the fountain, positioned precisely where you want the water to begin to flow.

3 Camouflage the tubing by carefully placing several small rocks over it. Without revealing its source, the water will cascade over the rock ledge and splash down on each slate stone.

LAY A DECK CARPET

Tools and materials
• DeckStrips by KT Industries (check www.deckstrip.com to compute how much you need) • gloves • pressure washer • utility knife or similar carpet-cutting tool • cutting mat • safety glasses • steel straight-edge or ruler • trash bag

1 Clean the deck and read all instructions. Cut the DeckStrips, as directed, starting with the longest pieces. DeckStrips have three separate peel-off backing strips; remove the center yellow strip to expose the adhesive.

2 Center the DeckStrip on a board and apply pressure to the middle section of the strip. Press down firmly along the length of the board. Discard the yellow strip, which is the removable peel-off backing.

3 Remove the two remaining clear peel-off backing strips. Press down firmly into place. Continue until you complete each board, following steps 1 and 2. Always start from the same side of the deck.

Garden Expansion

When Irene Jeruss moved into her new house in late 2003, she was careful to take her most prized possessions—her collection of plants—in the car with her. She left the china and crystal for the moving van. Irene, her husband, Jeff, and their children, Andrew and Sara, settled in Bristol, Connecticut, in a neo-Victorian house with no grass, trees, or flowers. Autumn was approaching; there was barely time to put the plants in the ground. But the following spring, Irene began to transform her barren lot into a cottage-style garden.

As a professional garden photographer, she had an eye for composition and color. Using rope and a garden hose, she established the outline of a border that would run from the front of the house to the end of the driveway. Once she had installed the anchor plants, including a dwarf Korean lilac and a "Bonica" shrub rose acquired from a local nursery, she divided the peonies and phlox she had brought with her, then moved on to small "filler" plants, with the idea of having as much color as possible from spring to fall. To enrich the predominantly sandy soil, she added plenty of compost and manure to the planting sites.

Soon her garden had expanded sufficiently to wrap around the house, with island beds that enclose the front yard for an intimate, cozy feeling. "There is always something beautiful in bloom here," she said. Her once-bare front yard became the envy of the neighborhood.

Before

ABOVE: When Irene and Jeff bought the house, it sat on bare ground. BELOW: Irene's "Knockout" rose brought a punch of bright color to her garden.

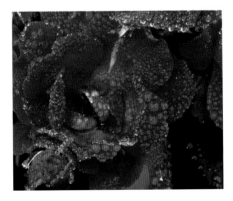

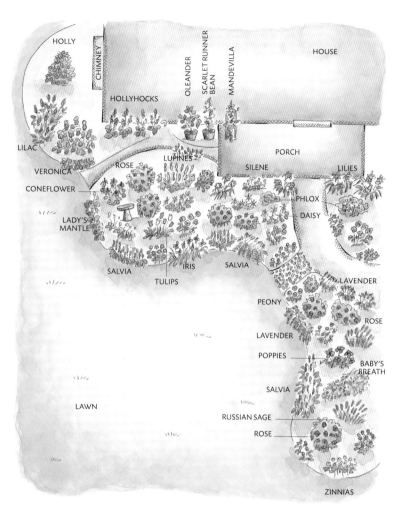

The garden plan labels: HOLLY, CHIMNEY, OLEANDER, SCARLET RUNNER BEAN, MANDEVILLA, HOUSE, HOLLYHOCKS, LILAC, VERONICA, CONEFLOWER, ROSE, LUPINES, SILENE, PORCH, LILIES, PHLOX, DAISY, LADY'S MANTLE, SALVIA, IRIS, TULIPS, SALVIA, LAVENDER, PEONY, ROSE, LAVENDER, POPPIES, BABY'S BREATH, SALVIA, RUSSIAN SAGE, ROSE, LAWN, ZINNIAS

ABOVE: Peonies are among Irene's favorite plants. She divides them in the fall and replants the divisions to increase their presence in her garden.

TOP: A cottage-style garden skirts the driveway and front walkway, hugging each corner of the house. Perennials are the main inhabitants, but annuals fill in to create a lush, full look. Mulched with shredded bark, the garden is a welcoming sight for visitors. Pots of vining plants and antique chairs complete the cottage theme. ABOVE: Irene's blue ageratum, red "Knockout" roses, white and yellow daisies, soft pink phlox, and peonies add up to a riot of pleasing color against the backdrop of the yellow house. LEFT: There is always something blooming in this expansive garden; when perennials stop blooming, annuals keep the show going.

Blooming Plans

Designer Dena Fishbein's world is filled with flowers. As host of the DIY Network series "Embellish This!", she parlayed her talent for transforming everyday objects into a range of stationery, fabrics, and decorative accessories sold in stores nationwide. Many of her designs have begun with stylized flowers and botanical patterns she painted herself. "There's something about a colorful bloom on a pillow or curtain that immediately lifts the spirits," she remarked.

Dena's designs are often inspired by the lush gardens that surround her Lafayette, California, home where she lives with Danny, her husband and business manager, and their three children. Since the mid-'90s, the couple have worked to improve their 75-year-old house while transforming its 5½-acre grounds into a showcase of outdoor rooms.

The Fishbeins really got serious about the design of their gardens when planning a family wedding. Working with landscape designer Laurie Callaway, they developed a master plan for their property based on the desire to create a series of separate gardens they could complete in stages. Edged with antique fencing, stone walls, arbors, and shrubbery, these spaces are dedicated to perennials, vegetables, herbs, and some one hundred roses.

As Dena is a perennial flea-market shopper, vintage architectural elements dot her home's outdoor spaces. Wrought-iron fencing encloses a vegetable garden, for example, while antique arbors and pergolas are the backbone for climbing roses. Also, an old chandelier hangs from the branch of an old tulip magnolia. Beneath it, on gold-hued gravel, sits an antique table and chairs. "It's so wonderful to create outdoor spaces that family and friends can discover as they meander through the yard," Dena explained. "The gardens really are extensions of our indoor rooms."

ABOVE: In the perennial beds, "Tuscan Blue" rosemary shrubs bracket clusters of delphinium, foxglove, coral bell, lamb's ear, iris, aster, and geranium. OPPOSITE: Roses climb along an antique arbor Dena found at a local flea market. Stone pavers create an informal pathway leading to the ivy-covered house. Throughout the gardens, Dena worked with a landscape designer to find just the right spots to place the birdbaths, birdhouses, fountains, statuary, and benches.

ABOVE: The colors of the plants in the window box were intentionally repeated in the striped seat cushions on the chair.

Bringing the Indoors Out

- Use old found objects like an iron gate or a length of railing found at a flea market as outdoor decorative accents
- Fill a birdbath with ivy or perennials, and use as an offbeat planter or path marker
- Group objects together to make a focal point. A collection of birdhouses mounted on the side of a barn or shed will catch the eye
- For an alfresco party, pull a rug onto the lawn and pile it with pillows to create comfortable spots where guests can sprawl and converse
- Don't forget the garden after dark. Plenty of lanterns, candles, and torches can fill it with a play of shadow and light

TOP: An iron fence from a flea market was painted to match the house's trim and staked with "Dream Weaver" climbing roses. ABOVE: A willow pergola filled with clematis and climbing roses anchors the center of the vegetable garden.

ABOVE: Callaway added wide, gracious steps to create a feeling of movement from the driveway to the upper lawn and the front of the house. A fountain found in France is a focal point, adding a touch of European elegance.

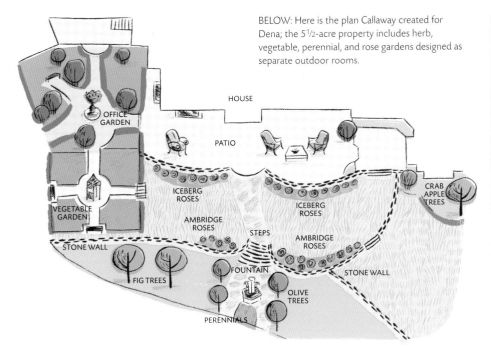

BELOW: Here is the plan Callaway created for Dena; the 5½-acre property includes herb, vegetable, perennial, and rose gardens designed as separate outdoor rooms.

HOUSE

OFFICE GARDEN

PATIO

VEGETABLE GARDEN

ICEBERG ROSES

ICEBERG ROSES

AMBRIDGE ROSES

STEPS

AMBRIDGE ROSES

STONE WALL

FIG TREES

FOUNTAIN

STONE WALL

CRAB APPLE TREES

OLIVE TREES

PERENNIALS

ABOVE: Surfaced with buckskin-hued flagstone, the patio was expanded to measure about 15 by 30 feet, running along one side the house as a comfortable space for relaxing and entertaining.

PERSONALIZE DECK CHAIRS

Tools and materials

- sandpaper
- exterior semi-gloss or high-gloss acrylic paint
- paint brushes
- wood primer
- wooden chairs
- ruler
- weatherproofing stain or finish

1 Sand away rough spots or knots on the chairs and then clean, rinse and leave them to dry. Apply primer, as directed, on each chair and let dry.

2 Brush on a base coat on each chair. After the paint dries lay down strips of masking tape vertically along the length of the chair, wherever you want the base color to show. Paint exposed areas the other color. Finish with a clear weatherproof coating.

How to Hire and Work with Contractors

For clients and contractors alike, every job is a risk. The client is always wondering, "Can this contractor get the job done? Will the job come in on budget? Will the work be finished on time?" And the contractor is always wondering, "Will I be paid when I need to be? Will hugely difficult problems arise? Will I be fired before I'm through?" There has to be a level of trust between contractor and client, and it's really up to the client before signing a contract to determine if the match is a good one.

Keep in mind that the contractor you hire should be someone you feel compatible with, someone you feel confident you can deal with. Always trust your instincts. If problems arise, as they inevitably do, you want a contractor who is responsive and responsible, someone you can talk things through with. If in doubt, ask yourself, "Is this person listening to me? Is this person asking me questions? Or is this person just an order-taker, someone who wants to tell me all he's ever done and what he thinks he wants to do?"

SIGNIFICANT SIGNS

The Remodelers Council of the National Association of Home Builders offers these helpful guidelines for finding and working with contractors:

1 **Know what you want.** Have a clear idea of the scope of your projected remodeling and, in order of importance, your priorities. The clearer you are in spelling out your needs, the less likely it is for misunderstandings to occur.
2 **Develop a budget.** Know how much money you can spend, and don't forget furnishings and landscaping, if they will be factors.
3 **Search wisely.** Ads in the newspaper or listings in the yellow pages may supply some contractor names, but your best candidates will be referrals from family, friends, or coworkers who have done successful remodelings. Other sources include home inspectors, suppliers of building materials, and local building-trades associations.
4 **Conduct interviews.** How well you communicate with the contractor

you are considering and how well that contractor communicates with you are important, but there are other points to consider: Does the contractor have a permanent mailing address and phone number—an e-mail address, voicemail system, cellphone or a pager? You want to hire someone who is established in the community, but also a person you can reach quickly, when necessary.

5 **Visit previous clients.** Verbal recommendations are important, and even the most positive ones might teach you something significant you did not expect to learn. However, the most important recommendations for contractor candidates are actual examples of their previous work. **Ask to visit one, two, or even three former job sites.** Satisfied home remodelers should be delighted to show off the improvements they have made. Your eyes should tell you how successful these improvements actually were, but take time to interview the homeowners and make some inquiries:
   - Did the project come in on or close to budget? Was it finished on or close to schedule? Was the job site kept clean?
   - Did the contractor return phone calls promptly? Would you hire this firm to do future work?
   - Note that contractors who try to discourage you from visiting previous clients could be questionable candidates.
6 **Do a character check.** You don't have to act like an FBI operative to find out if a contractor has paid his bills at the lumberyard or plumbing-supply store. A call to your local Better Business Bureau will tell you if your candidate has been the object of consumer complaints. And you can be very direct in asking if a contractor carries sufficient liability insurance to cover accidental property damage or injury to workers at the job site.
7 **Examine your bids carefully.** Ask for written bids and compare the numbers you receive. Know what each bid involves—the lowest may not be the best in every instance. If you lean toward

someone whose bid seems out of line, use your negotiating skills to help that contractor scale down a high number.

ALWAYS GET IT IN WRITING

Having a contract in writing is important; you should avoid working with anyone who says a simple handshake will do. A written, signed contract protects you as well as the contractor; it also sets forth exactly what your contractor is expected to do and when payments should be made.

A proper payment schedule will enable him or her to purchase the materials needed to do the work. You should know well in advance when such funds will be needed.

Most important, a contract is your insurance; an essential document if legal action is called for in the unlikely event of a default or a serious disagreement. It is also your only recourse if a contractor or subcontractor fails to complete the job satisfactorily. Mainly, however, the contract should include the following:
- What the contractor will and will not be responsible for.
- What materials will be used (product, size, color, brand name, and model).
- The total price, payment schedule, and any cancellation penalty.
- A "full" or "limited" warranty covering materials and workmanship for at least a year. (A "full" warranty means that money will be refunded in full unless faulty products are replaced or repaired to your satisfaction; a limited warranty means you should expect only partial refunds or replacements.)

Read the contract carefully. Make sure you understand it and that it covers everything you have requested. If you do not see a particular need spelled out, do not assume it is included; ask about it.

Never sign an incomplete agreement, and always keep a signed copy for your records. In most instances, a contractor will want to please you—if for no other reason than that he or she will want your recommendation in obtaining future business. Your relationship should be businesslike but not adversarial. That is why putting all of your needs in writing is the wisest, more responsible course to follow.

REALITY FACTORS

If you want a contractor to work within your budget, you have to indicate what your budget is. Of course, a great many people are reluctant to give out that figure, but a responsible contractor should know it. If it develops that more time must be spent in one area, perhaps he or she can suggest how to save money in another to compensate.

Money is usually as big an issue to the contractor as to the client, so it is up to you to suggest a payment schedule that will keep your contractor funded appropriately. If, for any reason, the contractor feels that money is being withheld, he may hold back on getting certain things done, because, of course, he won't hire subcontractors (framers, plumbers, electricians, roofers) if he can't afford to pay them. And without money up front, he can't buy materials either. Note that, depending on the size of your project, it's likely to cost 10 percent more than you expect, so you do need a cushion for unanticipated problems.

A good contractor can try to predict what problems might be encountered down the road, but, particularly in an old house, it is impossible to know ahead of time all the problems that might arise. Sometimes even a relatively new house can present remodeling problems. So, always be prepared for the unexpected.

One of remodeling's biggest budget-breakers is change. When clients change their minds, that slows jobs down, thus raising their cost.

Similarly, if something must be ripped out and redone, that can be really expensive. For your sake and your contractor's, plan carefully and know exactly what you want. Some changes are inevitable, but try and keep them to a minimum.

Overall, the contractor you hire should be sensitive to the fact that your house is not simply a job site but a home, and that having a crew of workmen in your home can be as intrusive as surgery. The ideal contractor should also be sensitive to the importance of communication.

If the person you hire is quick to return phone calls and willing to meet with you on demand, then you have someone who will be a solid teammate. That's important, because, no matter how big or small, a remodeling project is always a team effort.

Decoding the Codes

Building codes are written to protect the consumer, and most of the time they do, assuring a homeowner that the work being done is up to par.

THE BENEFITS

Codes also provide benefits that help ensure building safety. For example, without carefully written code requirements, there would be no legal recourse against a contractor who provides poor materials or workmanship. Further, in areas prone to natural disasters, strengthened codes increase the likelihood that homeowners can obtain insurance for their property. And building inspectors sometimes catch mistakes during construction that would be much costlier to correct after a job is completed.

THE BASICS

All building codes are based on federal standards that regulate materials and workmanship. The national guidelines, adopted long ago, are updated regularly to guarantee the long-term safety of new construction and remodeling projects.

LOCAL INPUT

By statute, every state, county, city, and town is entitled to adopt its own amendments and modifications to federal codes to reflect its own standards and needs (such as earthquake or hurricane reinforcement). It is the federal-local code combination to which a contractor must adhere when hired to remodel your home. Building permits are issued to make sure contractors meet or exceed local codes. Work done with a permit must be checked repeatedly by a local building inspector.

CORRECTABLE FAULTS

If the work is not up to code, a new certificate of occupancy will not be issued until all of the faults have been corrected. And without a valid certificate of occupancy, a house cannot be sold or occupied legally. Of course, no system is perfect. Some code writers are slow to change the regulations to reflect new materials being developed, and often

the code-setters are not as flexible or responsive as they could be.

In some cases, materials may be given the nod too quickly, before adequate testing is completed. Thus it pays to do enough basic research to become knowledgeable about the materials specified by your architect, contractor, or designer before signing off on the contract. Another potential problem is that an unscrupulous contractor might use the need for building-code inspection as an excuse for construction delays. Ideally, however, appointments with the building department can be made so far ahead of time that each completed phase can be inspected without slowing construction.

NO GUARANTEES

Any well-managed project should proceed according to a carefully laid-out schedule. Naturally, as with any regulations, building codes only work if enforced. And note that building departments do not indemnify their staff; you can't sue if an inspector errs. Thus, to be completely certain that your planned remodeling is up to code, consider bringing in an independent inspector to review construction after completion. Ultimately, you are the one responsible for the safety and livability of your home.

Permit Lore

Any home improvement project greater than a simple repair job requires a permit. Generally, work done within a home's existing footprint requires fewer permits than additions or other structural alterations. As regulations vary from area to area, it is important to contact your local building inspector to learn what you need to do before any work begins. The consequences of starting construction without a permit can be severe. Stiff fines may be imposed, and you could be forced to tear out any work that has already been done.

Giving a Home a New Face

There is nothing quite like the real thing—whether it's brick, stone, stucco, or wood—to give your home remodeling a finishing touch. But authenticity can come at a big price now. That is why other choices exist—factory-made materials that look authentic. Depending on where you live, some choices will be cheaper than others.

WOOD, THE WINNER

Wood is often regarded as the siding of choice, but not everyone can afford it. Prices vary around the country; so do available wood species. No matter where you live, you will find that beveled wood siding–tapered but similar to clapboards–comes in either smooth or rough textures. And it must be primed, then painted or stained.

Note that wood siding is never installed quickly, but not nearly as slowly as shingles or shakes, which go on singly, one course at a time. It is possible to cheat, however, and achieve the appearance of shingles in quicker- and easier-to-install panel form. Shakes are thicker than shingles at the butt end, and the sidewall exposure of shakes is usually greater, justifying their higher cost.

Tongue-and-groove siding, and the less formal board-and-batten siding, can be installed quickly, because each board covers a much larger area than that of shingles or shakes. Tongue-and-groove siding can be applied in patterns–vertically, horizontally, even diagonally; whereas boards with seams obscured by battens go on just vertically. Paint or stain will protect the surface.

WOOD-BASED MATERIALS

Plywood siding will last as long as other wood products if installed correctly and given adequate moisture protection. Plywood, which goes on fast—especially in panel form—comes in a variety of wood species, grades, and surface textures. Its price depends not only on its thickness but also on the quality of the top layer and the quantity of surface defects.

Hardboard, another popular wood derivative, is comparatively inexpensive, because it is made from refuse: wood chips turned into fibers no bigger than matchsticks. Under heat and extreme pressure, these fibers are mixed with additives to form panels or lap siding that imitate almost any surface. Although less than half the cost of clapboards, hardboard siding is weather resistant, long-lived if properly painted or finished, and convincingly woodlike in appearance.

OSB (oriented strand board) is also made from wood chips, flakes, or fibers, but arranged by grain in layers bonded together with resin. A siding material that often resembles rough-textured cedar, OSB was once used only as floor, wall, and deck sheathing. Manufacturers now consider it more stable than wood, however, and less likely to warp or crack.

MAN-MADE ALTERNATIVES

Vinyl mimics the look, if not the feel, of natural wood. Produced from extruded polyvinyl chloride, it is available in a wide variety of embossed textures and fade-resistant colors. Like corresponding wood products, it comes in various grades, but despite geographical price differences, it is not as costly as the wood it imitates. Vinyl siding can be applied horizontally or even vertically, but because it expands and contracts, it needs the freedom to move.

Aluminum siding, about twice the cost of vinyl, expands and contracts less, is more easily repainted, and is every bit as maintenance free. Unlike vinyl, however, it can be dented. Steel siding, nearly the same price as aluminum, is heavier, thus harder to install, but is recommended in areas where hefty hailstones could wreak havoc on aluminum surfaces.

THE MEASURE OF LONGEVITY

Quality manufacture is only one measuring stick of siding longevity. Among the others are the degree of exposure to weather change and sunlight, and the way the product is installed. Finally, applying appropriate maintenance procedures, as recommended by manufacturers, will ensure that whatever product you choose will have a good long life.

Making Sense of Floor Plans

The tubular package may arrive in protective cardboard or be tied with ribbon. Your bank and local building department will be receiving similar packages. Each contains a set of plans that must be approved before a remodeling project gets under way. The bank wants to make sure the work you do justifies the loan you requested; the building department will check for possible zoning violations. But the most important approval that is needed at this point is yours.

SPACE AND SCALE

A floor plan is basically a horizontal slice through a building, just as an elevation is a vertical slice. The horizontal slice shows where the walls go and how the spaces interrelate; the vertical slice shows how the windows and doors will affect the walls of each room. Construction plans are encyclopedic. Not only do they inform bankers and building inspectors, but, if really complete, they will tell the contractor and every subcontractor enough, so they will know how to get the job done.

Many pros believe it is important to provide reference points, drawing in a bed to help people see how large the bedroom will be. They might also show a sofa and a coffee table in a living room—not every piece of furniture, only the critical items to give the drawings some scale.

VISUAL AIDS

Construction drawings are normally produced to scale: one half inch to the foot. To fully grasp the spaces shown, you can cut out paper shapes—also to scale—that relate to your furnishings: piano, sofa, library table, whatever (or buy a plan book or kit with standard templates). Many builders and designers now also make use of computer aids, so that with a CAD (Computer Assistance Design) system, you can do a virtual walk-through of the new space.

Never leave anything to chance, however. Whether you use masking tape, paper cutouts, colored pencils, or a computer program, make sure you understand a plan thoroughly before you allow the first hammer blow to be struck.

Dealing with Problem Walls

Let's say you have a room whose old plaster walls have become cracked and unsightly. Maybe they were patched at some point, due to plumbing leaks or the need to repair faulty wiring. Or perhaps these wall surfaces were never smooth and always far from plumb. To improve them would be costly; painting them would only compound their unevenness; and wallpapering over them could become an optical nightmare of trying to match patterns when nothing squares up.

THE PANELING SOLUTION

One way out of the problem is to disguise it by paneling right over it—in effect, applying a false wall to the face of a troubled wall. Solid hardwood paneling can disguise flaws or enhance a wall surface. It can lighten or darken a room—and even make a ceiling appear higher or lower. Above all, the warm patina creates a comfortable "at home" feeling, whether your decorating style is traditional English, contemporary American, or eclectic.

Paneling is available in two categories: solid-board planks that come $1/4$- to $7/8$-inch thick, 3- to 12-inches wide, and 6- to 20-feet long, and also 4-by-8-inch panels, at the heart of which is either plywood or an engineered wood product, generally a high-density hardboard made of wood fibers bonded with adhesive under pressure to create a tough, springy sheet.

Wood paneling is no cure-all, of course. At best, it is a decorative cover-up. Some people like the look of grained wood, staining in tones that point up a particular decorating style. Others prefer using paint. Note that whitewashed and pickled hardwoods have grown in popularity for lighter, more casual-styled paneling.

OTHER PANELING PLUSES

There is more than one reason to consider paneling one or more walls of a room. Applied to the inside surface of an exterior wall, paneling gives you the opportunity to pack in additional insulation. Applied to an interior wall, it has noise-deadening value, reducing the amount of sound that may otherwise carry from one room to the next. As a decorating choice, solid wood paneling brings in new tone and texture that can totally alter the mood of a room.

When selecting a panel style, consider room size and the availability of natural light. Pale colors and smooth, continuous lines visually stretch small spaces; whereas darker tones and sharper divisions are more enclosing. A high-ceilinged room seems cozier when walls are textured with a planked finish. If you favor dark wood but are working with limited space, consider restricting dark tones to wainscoting or a single accent wall.

ADDING DECORATIVE DASH

Regardless of the style of your home or of the specific room or wall you want to panel, some type of molding will be needed as a finishing touch.

Hardwood moldings are an easy and economical way to add the richness of architectural detailing to a room, whether they are stained or painted to match your wall paneling or to provide a tonal contrast.

Wood moldings are available in literally hundreds of shapes and sizes—from simply streamlined strips to carved historic reproductions. They can be used to frame windows and doors effectively—and to offset whole walls, either as crown or baseboard moldings, or both. Oak, alder, beech, birch, cherry, maple, and walnut are among the most popular molding choices, and poplar can be an appealing option because it accepts paint so readily.

Moldings can be used to camouflage minor imperfections where a wall meets the ceiling, window, door, or floor. And baseboard moldings can be extremely effective in absorbing the hard knocks of everyday living—the bump of a vacuum cleaner, for example, or repeated buffeting by a child's runaway toy. In addition, molding strips give a finished look to any cabinetry you may include as part of your paneled wall design. Traditionally, moldings used as chair rails have a practical as well as decorative impact in dining and breakfast rooms. Nail them anywhere from 32 to 42 inches above the floor, the point at which chairs would be most likely to hit the wall. Also known as running rail, this molding comes in a wide variety of widths and styles.

Beautifying with Faux Finishes

If you want a special look on walls or woodwork, consider the vast potential of paint. There are decorative paint techniques that will help you enhance a surface or, if necessary, disguise a problem. Keep in mind that decorative painting is an art, not a science—which means some of the most impressive results can be achieved not through strict adherence to a formula but through experimentation and improvisation. Basically, there are two types of paint: latex (or water-based) and alkyd (oil-based). Both can be used to create handsome faux finishes, but note that latex cannot be applied over oil. To confirm how a surface was previously painted, soak the tip of a cotton swab in rubbing alcohol and scrub a small out-of-sight painted area. If the paint comes off or becomes sticky, it's water-based. If not, it's oil-based.

WASHES AND GLAZES

A wash is, quite simply, a thinned paint that gives a surface the illusion of texture. Depending upon the precise look you envision, the paint can be thinned a little or a lot (but mixing 2 or 3 parts water with 1 part paint works well in most situations). A wash produces color that appears fresher, purer, and more delicately textured than what a glaze produces.

A glaze is usually a thinned paint applied over a tinted base coat to produce a finish more translucent than a wash can achieve. A glaze can give a surface a rich, dark glow. There are various ways to create this look. One effective way is to mix 1 part glazing liquid with 1 part paint plus 1 part thinner (or latex extender if you use latex paint). Glazing liquid is an important component of many faux-finish techniques. Adding glaze to paint slows down drying time, making it easier for the paint to be manipulated.

Applying glaze makes paint translucent, allowing the base coat to show through.

In determining whether to use a wash or a glaze, consider the complexity of the project and the visual effect you want. Glazes dry more slowly than washes, and remain workable longer. Washes are easier to make, modify, and clean up.

COLOR-WASHING

Color-washing produces a translucent effect that involves building up very thin layers of paint to create a textured-looking finish. The simplest method starts with brushing on a solid-color base coat, which becomes the background color. After it dries completely, use a paintbrush to apply small, irregular patches of thin wash (the thinner the wash, the lighter the color). Applying a color-wash to a base-coated surface with a bunched-up rag is called ragging-on. It achieves a textured effect because the rag actually pulls off some of the color.

Color-washing can produce attractive results even if just one color is used. But any number of successive coats of wash can be applied, as long as you allow each coat to be fully dry before brushing on the next one. If, however, you plan to apply several coats of wash, be sure to leave enough base coat showing so that your background color is still visible when the job is done.

SPONGING

Use this decorative painting technique to create a mottled, irregular pattern. Either solid-color paint or washes can be sponged on or off a surface. And you can use two or more colors—just be sure to let each one dry completely before applying the next one. Here are the basic steps to follow:

1 Apply a solid base coat of paint to the surface, typically in a light shade.
2 Lightly moisten a natural sponge with water, then dip sparingly into the second color.
3 Starting in the center of a surface, gently tap your sponge against that surface, turn the sponge frequently, and change directions to create a variegated pattern.
4 When you have achieved the desired effect in the center, work outward toward the corners or edges.

COMBING

Combing is one of the most popular faux-painting techniques for walls, also one of the most challenging. Variations include stria, burlap, gingham, and bead-board patterns, all done with an appropriate combing tool, which is notched and made of either rubber or cardboard. Here is a basic technique: (You can also achieve a striated look by dragging a very stiff brush or a piece of steel wool across a wet-painted surface.)

1 Start with walls that are clean, dry, and dull-surfaced. Firmly mask off all woodwork, then apply a base coat of latex paint in an eggshell or satin finish, and let dry for at least four hours.
2 Once your starting wall has been painted, mask off the corners of adjacent walls to prevent the smearing of glaze.
3 For the glaze, mix 1 part satin-finish paint with 5 parts latex glazing liquid, and stir well. With a paintbrush and a top-quality ¼-nap roller, thinly and evenly apply about two roller widths of glaze at a time.
4 With your combing tool, apply even pressure while pulling the tool downward through the glaze—for a basic "combed" look. To eliminate drips caused by glaze buildup, clean the combing tool on a cotton rag after each pass through the wet glaze. If you need to redo a section, simply reroll the area while still wet, then re-comb.

STIPPLING

Choose this technique if you want a "broken" wall color, one more subtly textured than what you would achieve by sponging. The look is suedelike rather than mottled or dappled, and the surface has greater depth than when covered with a flat color. Stippling adds richness to a finish by breaking a wall color into a mass of very small dots. The only special tool you may need is a large, soft-bristled stippling brush available from a paint or artist's supply retailer. Here is the three-step process:

1 Apply a solid-color base coat in the usual way: any color, light or dark.
2 After the base coat dries, applying your top coat, moving from one end of a wall to the other in foot-wide strips.
3 Working swiftly, before any paint strips dry, stab at the wet paint with your stippling brush to remove some of the paint you just applied. Keep your brush absorbent by periodically blotting off as much excess paint as possible.

Stippling usually involves just two colors of paint or wash, but you can incorporate additional colors simply by stippling them on rather than off. With stippling, as with any technique, you should practice on a sample board before tackling the surfaces in a room.

Glossary

AC: Alternating current, which is standard household current, so called because it reverses direction at a regular frequency—in North America 60 times per second; in Europe, 50.

ALLEN WRENCH: A hexagonal, rod-shaped tool designed for turning allen screws, which have hexagonal depressions in each head.

AMP: Short for "ampere," the amount of electrical current that flows through a circuit—wire or other conductor—at any given time. Household electrical circuits are rated by the number of amps.

BALUSTERS: Spindles or other vertical members that help support a staircase railing.

BASEBOARD: A board or molding, available in a wide variety of sizes and styles, that is installed where a wall meets the floor.

BATT: A precut section of fiberglass or rock-wool insulation.

BATTENS: Narrow pieces of wood applied over the joints of wider pieces, as in board-and-batten installations.

BEAD: A continuous strip or length of caulk, glue, adhesive, or similar substance.

BEAM: A length of lumber or metal used as a horizontal support in construction.

BEARING WALL: An interior or exterior wall that helps support roof or floor joists above it.

BEVEL: The end of a piece of wood or other material that has been cut at an angle.

BOND: The pattern in which bricks or other masonry units are laid; also, the cementing action of an adhesive.

BONDING AGENT: In tile, plaster, and masonry work, a chemical that helps one material adhere better to another.

BTU: The British Thermal Unit is the amount of heat needed to raise one pound of water one degree Fahrenheit.

BULLNOSE: A tile or board with a blunt, rounded edge, used for finishing exposed edges or corners.

BUTT HINGE: A type of hinge that is attached to the edge of a door and the face of a jamb so that, when the door closes, only the knuckles of the hinge are exposed.

BUTT JOINT: A joint formed by the meeting of two square-cut pieces of wood.

CANTILEVER: A beam or beams projecting beyond a support member.

CASEMENT WINDOW: Window whose sash is designed to swing open outward by means of a crank-type hardware system.

CASING: Molding applied like a picture frame to trim door and window openings.

CEMENT: A mineral powder used as an ingredient in concrete and mortar; also, any type of adhesive.

CENTERSET FAUCET: A faucet whose handles and spout are contained in a single unit, usually installed directly above a sink's center.

CHAIR RAIL: Horizontal molding placed on a wall at chair-back height.

CHAMFER: A small bevel cut along the edge of a piece of wood.

CHIMNEY CAP: The mortar or concrete top of a chimney surrounding the flue pipe.

CIRCUIT: The path of an electrical current from its source all the way through various components, such as lighting, then back to the source.

CIRCUIT BREAKER: A protective switch that automatically shuts off the flow of electricity when the amount of current exceeds a predetermined amperage

CLAPBOARD: Historic description of horizontal beveled siding whose boards overlap.

CONCRETE: A hard material, used for building and paving, made of a mix of cement, sand and/or gravel, and water.

CORNICE: The horizontal molding around the top of a wall; also a wood frame, upholstered or covered, mounted at the top of draperies.

COUNTERSINK: To drive in a screw or nail so the head lies just below the surface.

COURSES: Rows or layers of material, such as bricks in a wall or shakes or shingles on a roof.

CRAWL SPACE: The area under a house lacking a basement.

CROWN MOLDING: A decorative molding installed in the area where wall meets ceiling.

DADO: The wall space between a baseboard and chair rail.

DAMPER: A movable steel flap that closes a chimney flue or ventilating duct to keep outside air from entering a home.

DC: Direct current, so called because its flow is constant in one direction; the type of current produced by a battery.

DORMER: An extension of a home's upstairs space, often an attic, that extends out from the main roof.

DOUBLE-GLAZED WINDOW: A window that has a thermal barrier, often sealed in the sash between inner and outer sets of glass panes and separated by air or an inert gas such as orgon.

DOUBLE-HUNG WINDOW: A window with two sashes, one above the other; both the top and bottom sashes can usually be slid up and down within the frame.

DOWEL: A short, thin, round stick of wood that is inserted into a matching hole bored in an adjacent piece to strengthen a wood joint.

DOWNSPOUT: Vertical pipe made of metal or plastic that carries water down to the ground from a roof gutter.

DRYWALL: A basic interior building material comprising big sheets of pressed gypsum faced with heavy paper on both sides; also known as wallboard, plasterboard, gypsum board, and by the trade name Sheetrock.

DUCT: A pipe that carries air from a furnace or air conditioner to a home's living areas, or carries exhaust air from a fan or ventilator.

EFFLORESCENCE: A whitish powder, often exuded by the mortar joints in masonry work, that accumulates when salts rise to the surface.

EPOXY: A type of adhesive that is durable and extremely strong.

FASCIA BOARD: Horizontal trim that forms the face of a cornice or the eave of a roof.

FIREBRICK: Extremely heat-resistant brick used to line boilers and fireplaces.

FLANGE: A steel rim that allows one object to be attached to another one.

FLASHING: Metal, roofing felt, or composition strips used to seal seams between roofing and other surfaces, applied to keep water out.

FLUE: A pipe or other channel that carries smoke and combustion gases to the outside air.

FOOTING: The base on which a masonry wall rests.

FRENCH DOOR: An in-swinging door with rectangular glass panes extending its full length, also called a garden door.

FROST LINE: The lowest depth at which the ground can be expected to freeze in a particular place, it determines the minimum depth of foundation footings and basement wall insulation.

FURRING: Lightweight wood or metal strips that even up a wall or ceiling for a drywall or paneling installation.

GABLE: The triangular part of an exterior wall formed by two sloping roof angles.

GLAZING: Glasswork, also the process of installing glass.

GLAZING COMPOUND: A thick, waterproof caulk used to seal the joint between a window's glass and frame.

GRADE: Ground level, or the elevation at any given point.

GRAIN: The direction in which wood fibers or fabric threads flow.

GRAINING: Using paint or other finishing materials to artificially simulate wood grain.

GROUT: Mortar that has been thickened with water to a consistency enabling it to flow into the joints of tile or masonry and fill them solidly.

GYPSUM BOARD: See drywall.

HARDBOARD: A synthetic wood product made by chemically converting wood chips to fibers, then forming panels under heat and high pressure.

HARDWOOD: The wood of broad-leafed, often deciduous trees, such as oak, maple, cherry, and alder; the designation does not reflect actual wood hardness or density.

HEADER: A horizontal member placed over an opening, such as a door or window, to support the framing members above it; also a beam used to support the ends of joists.

HIP: The convex angle formed when two sloping roof sections meet, usually at a 90-degree angle to each other.

HVAC: Heating, ventilating, and air conditioning systems that are often grouped together in a single, complex mechanism.

INSULATION: A non-conducting material used to prevent the transfer of heat, sound, or electricity across or through a surface.

JALOUSIE: A type of window made up of narrow horizontal planes that pivot together and overlap slightly when closed.

JAMB: The pieces that form the visible framework of an opening, such as that for a door or window.

JOINT COMPOUND: A thick paste used in conjunction with drywall tape to seal and conceal joints between sheets of drywall.

JOIST: Any one of a group of parallel horizontal boards set on edge and parallel to each other, to support a floor or ceiling.

LACQUER: A clear, durable, solvent-based, moisture-resistant wood finish.

LAMINATE: Two or more surfaces bonded compressed under great pressure and bonded, such as plywood or plastic laminate.

LATH: Thin, narrow strips of wood, gypsum, or metal fastened to rafters, joists, or studs to form a support for plaster, slate, stucco, or tile.

LATTICE: A thin, flat molding, rectangular in profile, used to build latticework or conceal button joints.

LINTEL: A load-bearing beam over an opening in masonry, such as a door or fireplace.

LOW-E GLASS: Low-emissivity glass, which has a coating on one side or a film suspended between two panes or a microscopically thin layer of metal oxides; each will deflect heat but admit visible light.

LOW-VOLTAGE LIGHTING: Lighting that operates on power-saving 12-volt and often 24-volt current rather than the standard 120 volts.

MASONRY: A construction made of stone, bricks, concrete blocks, poured concrete, or similar materials.

MITER: A joint formed by beveling the ends or edges of two pieces at 45-degree angles, then joining them to make a 90-degree angle.

MOLDING: Decorative strips or sections of wood, tile, plastic, or other material that are used primarily to conceal a joint.

MORTAR: A thick cement-based substance that, when hardened, is useful in holding bricks and other forms of masonry in place.

MORTISE: A hole, slot, groove, or other recess into which another element fits—hinges, for example, so they lie flush.

MULLION: The vertical divider between the windows in a building that has two or more windows.

MUNTIN: A strip of wood that divides a window sash into separate panes.

NEWEL: The main post at the foot of a stairway, or the central support of a spiral or winding flight of stairs.

PARTICLEBOARD: A form of composite board or paneling formulated of pressed wood chips bonded with some form of adhesive.

PIANO HINGE: A hinge with a thin barrel that extends the entire length of the parts to be made movable, as the lid of a grand piano.

PIER: A masonry post that serves as a footing for a wood or steel post.

PLASTERBOARD: See drywall.

PLUMB: Vertically level, perfectly perpendicular to a floor or other horizontal surface.

PLYWOOD: A building panel made by gluing thin layers of wood together; to ensure strength, grain directions alternate, layer to layer.

POINTING: Filling and finishing the mortar joints of brickwork.

POLYURETHANE: A synthetic varnish that is clear, non-yellowing, hard, fast drying, and resistant to wear, water, and alcohol.

POST: A vertical support member that is usually made of one piece of lumber or a metal pipe or I-beam.

POST-AND-BEAM: A basic building method that utilizes relatively few sturdy posts and beams to support an entire structure.

PRESSURE-BALANCING VALVE: An anti-scald tub and shower valve that senses the water pressure of the hot- and cold-water inlets and maintains the desired balance despite abrupt water pressure changes.

PRESSURE-TREATED LUMBER: Lumber that is rot-resistant because chemical preservatives are injected into it under pressure; used in outdoor situations where the wood may be in contact with the ground, rainwater, concrete, or masonry.

PRIMER: A special paint created to properly seal a surface and provide good adhesion for the application of wallpaper or the finish coat of paint.

PVC: Polyvinyl chloride; a rigid plastic used for plumbing pipe systems.

RABBET: A square channel, groove, or recess cut along the edge of a board.

RAFTER: Any of the parallel framing members that support the roof of a building.

RAIL: Any relatively lightweight horizontal element to be used in fence building or as a horizontal section between panels in a paneled door.

RISER: The upright piece between two stair steps; in plumbing, the supply tube that connects a faucet to its shut-off valve.

ROUGHING-IN: The initial stage of a plumbing, electrical, carpentry, or other project.

R-VALUE: A measure of the resistance an insulating material offers to heat transfer; the higher the R-value, the more effective the insulation.

SADDLE: The plate, sometimes called a threshold, at the bottom of some door openings.

SASH: The framework of a window into which panes of glass are mounted.

SETBACK: The distance, determined by local building codes, that a structure must be built from property lines.

SETTLEMENT: Shifts in a structure, usually caused by underground freeze-and-thaw cycles.

SHAKE: A thick wood shingle, usually edge-grained.

SHEATING: The first covering on a roof or exterior wall, usually fastened directly to rafters or studs.

SHIM: A thin, flat, or wedge-shaped piece of wood used to support or level an object during installation.

SHIPLAP SIDING: Horizontal wood siding whose boards are rabbeted so the bottom edges lap over the edges of adjacent boards and create a flush joint.

SILL: A horizontal piece that forms the base of a structural frame, such as a window.

SINGLE-HUNG: A window with two sashes, one above the other, in which only one sash can be raised or lowered.

SLEEPERS: Boards laid directly over a masonry slab to support a wood subfloor.

SOFFIT: The underside of a roof overhang, often covered with a panel that has small openings as vents; also the dropped section of a ceiling that may conceal obstructions.

SOFTWOOD: The wood of conifers such as Douglas fir, pine, and redwood, but having nothing to do with the wood's hardness.

SOLID SURFACING: A type of tough, man-made countertop material formulated to have the same color and texture throughout its thickness.

SPACKLING COMPOUND: A pastelike substance used to repair cracks and small holes in drywall before a wall is primed.

STACK: A vertical pipe that serves as a bathroom's main plumbing vent and drain.

STILE: A vertical component of a structure such as a door or cabinet front.

STUCCO: A brittle, durable, cement-based material used to form a hard finish on exterior walls.

STUD: A vertical framing member to which sheathing, drywall, paneling, and other finish material may be affixed.

SUBFLOOR: Sheets of plywood or other sturdy material that extend under all the walls of a frame house and onto which the underlayment and finish flooring are laid.

SUBSTRATE: Backing material applied before a tile or laminate counter goes on.

TACK CLOTH: A porous rag so impregnated with varnish as to be relatively sticky; it is used to remove dust and sanding residue from a surface before finishing work is done.

TEMPLATE: A pattern or mold to guide the cutting or shaping of material, such as a countertop.

TENON: A protrusion cut into one part of a joint to fit a matching mortise in the second part of the joint.

TONGUE-AND-GROOVE: Interlocking siding or flooring boards, each with a narrow projection milled along one edge that fits into a matching groove along the edge of the next board.

TREAD: The level part of a staircase.

TRUE: Accurately formed or constructed; straight, flat, or level.

TRUSS: An assembly of wood or metal members that creates a strong framework; it is often used instead of rafters and joists to support a roof or floor.

UL: Underwriters' Laboratories, an independent testing agency that checks electrical and other components for possible safety hazards.

UNDERLAYMENT: The material placed under the finish coverings of roofs or floors to provide waterproofing.

VALLEY: A roof depression formed when two sloping roof segments converge.

VAPOR BARRIER: A sheet of plastic or other nonporous material that retards the movement of water vapor through walls, floors, and ceilings.

VARNISH: Any of a variety of tough, clear, durable liquid wood finishes that resists water, heat, and alcohol.

VENEER: A thin layer of beautifully grained wood or other material that is applied to the top of an interior surface, such as a table.

VOLT: The amount of force needed or used to push electricity through a wire.

WAINSCOTING: Decorative paneling, usually made of wood, that covers only the lower portion of a wall.

WALLBOARD: See drywall.

WATT: The quantity of electricity being used at any given moment. The number of watts is determined by multiplying volts times amps.

WEATHER STRIPPING: A long, thin, flexible length of waterproof material used to seal gaps around the edges of doors and windows to block out moisture and drafts.

Photo credits

Cover: William P. Steele; back cover, top to bottom: Hunter Breedlove, Rob Karogis (2), Linda Hanselman; pages 6–9, 10 top, 11: Linda Hanselman; page 10 bottom: Balmer Architectural Interior Mouldings; pages 12–15: Claudio Santini; page 16: Tria Giovan; pages 17–21: Gridley & Graves; pages 22–25: Rob Karogis; pages 26–29: Hunter Breedlove; pages 30–33: Rob Karogis; pages 34–38: Deborah Ory; pages 39–41: Claudio Santini; page 43 bottom: Brian Vanden Brink; pages 44–47: William P. Steele; page 48: John O'Hagan for Lowe's; page 49: Home Depot Style Ideas; pages 50–51: Edmund Barr; pages 52–54: Liz Glasgow; page 55 top, bottom center: Norwall Group, Inc.; pages 56–57: Mark Lund; page 58: Olson Photographic LLC; pages 60–61: Olson Photographic LLC; pages 62–64: Peter Ledwith; pages 65–67: Ron Holt; pages 68–70: Robert Reck; pages 72–74: Robert Polett; page 75: Glidden; page 76–78: Matthew Milman; pages 79–80: Peter Vanderwarker; pages 81–83: Alex Hauden; pages 84–86: Kate Roth; page 87: Glidden; page 88: Nick Novelli; page 89: Olson Photographic LLC; page 90: George Lambros; page 91, top left: Dutchboy; page 91, top right: Brass Light Gallery; page 91, bottom: Kaskel Architectural Photography; page 92, top: Mark Samu; page 92, bottom: Glenn A. Grube; page 92, top to bottom: Lutron, Hubbardton Forge, Seagull Lighting (2); pages 94–96: Gridley & Graves; pages 97–99: Erica George Dines Photography; page 100: Greg Hardley; page 102: Philip Wegener; pages 103–104: Brad Daniels; pages 105–106: Paul Crosby; pages 107–109: Ryan Benyi; pages 110–111: David Papazian; page 112: Rosemarie Stiller; page 113: Dana Wheelock; pages 114–115: Bill Enos; pages 116–117: Greg Hardley; pages 118–119: Robin Stubbert; pages 120–121: Melabee M. Miller; pages 122–123: Lowe's Creative Ideas for Your Home; page 124, top: Gridley & Graves; page 124, bottom: Anne Gummerson; page 125: Anne Gummerson; page 126, bottom left: Brian Vanden Brink; page 126, bottom right: Ken Chen; page 127 top: Robin Stubbert; page 127 bottom: Jim Fiora; page 129: Lydia Cutter Photography; pages 130–131: David Papazian; page 135: Glidden; pages 136–137: Lydia Cutter Photography; page 140: Albert Laus; page 141: Mark Citret; pages 142–143: Gridley & Graves; page 144: Erich Hanson; page 145, top: Beckett; pages 146–147: Irene Jeruss; pages 148–150: David Duncan Livingstone.

Acknowledgments

The author appreciates the efforts of editorial colleagues Leslie Clagett, Kitty Cox, Karen Walden, Peter Walsh, and Barbara Winfield for having published such incisive, informative magazine material, which became the source of this book. Thanks also to Matthew Levinson for thorough and comprehensive photo research, and especially to Olivia Monjo, Editor-in-Chief of Woman's Day Special Interest Publications, for saying yes to the idea for a book on this topic. Undying gratitude is also expressed to publisher Dorothée Walliser, who supplied the inspiration, the impetus, and the wherewithal to see to this book's publication. She is a rarity in publishing today, one of few book editors who actually reads—and edits—what she publishes.